Good Governance in India

By the Same Editors

- Globalization and Religion: Interactions and Divergences.
- Secularism and Pluralistic Democracy in India.
- Electroral Participation of Muslim Women in India: A Comparative Study.

About the Editors

Dr. (Mrs.) Vasundhara Mohan, Ph.D. in Political Science from the Rajasthan University, Jaipur (India), worked at the Centre of Soviet Studies (later renamed Centre for Central Eurasian Studies) of the University of Mumbai for over 23 years, teaching Soviet foreign Policy, Nationalities and International Relations at the post-graduate level and guided research. After her retirement from the University of Mumbai as Associate Professor, she was associated with the Centre for Study of Society and Secularism founded by Late Dr. Asghar Ali Engineer in Mumbai for over 8 years. She is presently associated with the Institute of Indian Culture, Mumbai since 2014 as Programme Director.

She is the author of several books and has contributed to edited volumes. An Alumna of Salzburg Seminar, she participated in the 3rd International Women's Peace Conference in Dallas TX (USA) in 2007. She has presented a paper on the Political participation of Muslim women in India at the International Workshop held at Hildesheim (Germany). She is the author of Political Participation of Muslim Women in India: A Comparative Study (Concept Publishing Company Pvt. Ltd., New Delhi, 2018). She has also published a number of articles on Muslim women in Indian journals.

Scaria Pannackal is the Director of the Institute of Indian Culture, a Research Centre for the study of Culture, Religion and Society. He has his Doctorate in Social Philosophy from the University of Pune. He has published Articles on various aspects of Culture and Religion. Presently, he also teaches at St. Xavier's College, Mumbai.

Good Governance in India

Prospects and Challenges

Edited by
Vasundhara Mohan
Scaria Pannackal

CONCEPT PUBLISHING COMPANY PVT. LTD.
NEW DELHI-110059

ISBN-13: 978-93-86682-73-4

First Published 2019

Published and Printed by

Concept
Since 1974

Concept Publishing Company Pvt. Ltd.
A/15-16, Commercial Block, Mohan Garden,
New Delhi-110059 (India)
T : 91 11 25351460, 91 11 25351794
E : publishing@conceptpub.com, *W*: www.conceptpub.com

Cataloging in Publication Data--Courtesy: D.K. Agencies (P) Ltd. <docinfo@dkagencies.com>

National Seminar on Good Governance in India (2017 : Mumbai, India)
Good governance in India : prospects and challenges / edited by Vasundhara Mohan, Scaria Pannackal.
pages cm
"This book is a compilation of papers presented by reputed academicians at the 2-day National Seminar on Good Governance in India organised by the Institute of Indian Culture, Mumbai on 1-2 April, 2017"--About the book.
Includes bibliographical references and index.
ISBN 9789386682734

1. India--Politics and government--21st century--Congresses. 2. Transparency in government--India--Congresses. 3. India--Social policy--Congresses. 4. India--Economic policy--Congresses. I. Mohan, Vasundhara, 1947- editor. II. Pannackal, Scaria, editor. III. Institute of Indian Culture (Mumbai, India), organizer. IV. Title.

LCC JQ231.N38 2017 DDC 320.954 23

Preface

India is in the throes of a fierce passion for governance, not merely any governance but 'maximum governance' and 'minimum government'. India has been celebrating 'Good Governance Day' on 25th December each year since 2014. Ever since Narendra Modi took over as the Prime Minister, nobody speaks of the need for good government any more; only good governance.

Although, the features of a good governance were first enunciated by Kautilya, in the modern era, the term 'governance' was first used by the World Bank in its 1989 report on African Economies. In defining governance, the World Bank, said that it is "the exercise of political power to manage a nation's affairs." For the World Banket did not matter whether a given country had a democracy or a dictatorship. What mattered was an efficient management. The World Bank 'governance' model includes elements of a liberal democracy, accountability etc. For this, it is necessary to first create a demand for good governance.

The present NDA government, headed by Narendra Modi, is invested with the mandate to give India a Good Governance. The agenda before the government is too big and it remains to be seen how far it would be successful in carrying out its mandate.

Besides the government, the executive and judicial arms of the government, the society at large and the Non-Governmental Organisations (NGOs) should be equally determined to help the government in the process of giving good governance. For, accountability, transparency, empowerment, and citizen participation are the key elements of Modi's 'good governance' agenda.

In keeping with Institute's tradition of organising seminars on contemporary topics, the two-day seminar was organised by the Institute of Indian Culture with a view to discussing the various facets of Good Governance and the role and participation of the society, judiciary and NGOs in the process.

Acknowledgements

The two-day national seminar on 'Good Governance' was organised with financial support from the Indian Council of Social Science Research, Government of India, New Delhi. ICSSR's support enabled us to invite reputed scholars from outside Mumbai. The Institute of Indian Culture gratefully acknowledges the constant support of the ICSSR.

We would also like to thank the various scholars, who made it convenient to participate in the Seminar and present papers on the various facets of Good Governance. We are thankful to Fr. Dr. M.K. George, former Director of Indian Social Institute, Bangalore and Professor Laxmikant Dwivedi, Principal, SVKM's Pravin Gandhi College of Law, Mumbai, who played key roles in the orgnisation of the Seminar.

We acknowledge with thanks the support extended by Professor Michael Sebastian and Dr. M.T. Joseph in organising the seminar. We also acknowledge the support extended by research scholars Dr. (Mrs.) Bindu Chaturvedi, and Mr. Anwar Hussain.

Dr. (Mrs.) Vasundhara Mohan
Dr. Scaria Pannackal

Contents

List of Contributors

Dr. Arpita Shah (Ms.), Assistant Professor, CHBSNDT Women's University, Churchgate, Mumbai-400020

Dr. John Solomon Gaikwad, Professor, Department. of Anthropology, Savitribai Phule, Pune University, Pune-411007.

Dr. Laxmikant Dwivedi, Principal, SVKM's Pravin Gandhi College of Law, Vile Parle West, Mumbai-400056.
E-mail: svkm.pgcl@gmail.com

Dr. Leela D'Souza, Faculty, Institute of Indian Culture, Mumbai-400093.
E-mail : leelads2005@yahoo.co.in

Dr. M.K. George, formerly Director, Indian Social Institute, Bangalore.
E-mail: gmutholil@gmail.com

Dr. Manisha Madhava, Associate Professor, Department of Political Science, SNDT Women's University, Mumbai-400020.
E-mail: m.manisha@gmail.com

Nirmal Dhanasamy, Research Scholar, Mumbai University.
E-mail: nimmysvd@gamil.com

Dr. P.M. Kamath, formerly Professor of Politics, Department of Civics and Politics, Mumbai University Vidyanagari, Santacruz-East, Mumbai.
E-mail: pmkamath11@gmail.com

Dr. Prashant Bansode, Associate Professor, Gokhale Institute of Politics and Economics, Pune.
E-mail: prashantsoc@gmail.com

Dr. R.R. Patil, Associate Professor, Department of Social Work, Jamia Millia Islamia, New Delhi-110025.
E-mail: ravi_patil72@yahoo.com

Dr. Ravindra Singh, Assistant, Professor, Department of Social Work, Dr. Bhim Rao Ambedkar College, University of Delhi, Delhi.
E-mail: singhravi30@gmail.com

Dr. Scaria Pannackal, Director, Institute of Indian Culture, Mumbai-400093.
E-mail: spannackalsvd@rediffmail.com

Dr. Vasundhara Mohan, Programme Director, Institute of Indian Culture, Mumbai-400093.
E-mail : mohan_rallapalli@hotmail.com

Dr. Vibhuti Patel, Professor and Head, PG Department of Economics, SNDT Women's University, Churchgate, Mumbai-400020.
E-mail : vibhuti.np@gmail.com

Introduction

Independent India is being governed by its own leaders since 1947. During the last over seven decades, India has witnessed a variety of leaders, some of whom gave the country good governance through good leadership. A "good leadership" is a fundamental prerequisite for good governance and for the achievement of the ideals professed in the Constitution of Secular Democracy like India, where a number of religions co-exist. The major factors that reflect the quality of governance are social justice and equality of rights and opportunities, among others. Though these concepts already exist in the Constitution of India, it is in ensuring the enjoyment of the constitutional guarantees by all sections of the people that the competency of the leadership lies and the nature of governance is determined.

Governance in India

India is world's largest and most vibrant democracy. The concept of governance was decisively shaped by the freedom movement led by Mahatma Gandhi and the aspirations of the founding fathers of the Constitution. While every nation is guided by certain values, w0hich are shared by the people and the government, national commitment to such values greatly influence the content and quality of governance. In the Indian context, at the time of the inauguration of the Republic, these values were nationalism, democracy, secularism, non-alignment and mixed economy.

Indian people have shown tremendous confidence in democratic system of governance. Drafters of the Constitution of India established a democratic society and acknowledged its significance by giving constitutional status to the Election Commission of India.

The Supreme Court of India has regarded democracy as one of the basic features of the Constitution of India.

Indian leaders took a historic decision to make India a secular state notwithstanding the partition of India on religious lines. Though, there is no State religion, safeguards were built in the Constitution to protect religious and educational institutions of religious minorities and allow them enjoy their personal laws in religious matters, although a Uniform Civil Code became a Directive Principle for the State. Though, religion always had a major place in the private lives of the citizens, politicisation of religious, ethnic and caste ties have reached unprecedented levels. Communal and sectarian approaches have become more prominent in Indian polity and also in public policy formulations at the national and state levels.

In the initial years of Independence, the executive functioned with considerable autonomy in hearing and solving public grievances, maintenance of public order particularly in case of ethnic and communal disturbances and enjoyed considerable discretion in implementation of land reforms and community development projects. But, over a period, the hold of politicians began to be affected with demands for allocation of scarce resources in favour of ruling elites and powerful interest groups. The State gradually started shedding its neutral stance in dealing with demands. The 'neutrality' of the civil service came under stress due to political interference. The fragmentation of the authority at the Centre characterised by coalition governments since the late 1980s has only deepened and extended these processes. But, after each election, common people have started asserting their voice, changing their representatives in the States and also at the Centre. This phenomenon, supported by the civil society groups, the media and an active judiciary has ushered in demands for accountability of the executive.

In view of the above situation, a need has been felt to further strengthen democracy. Various measures are being explored to make democracy more participatory. But, participatory democracy has to be accompanied by good governance if the former were to be strengthened. There is a growing consensus that both governments and citizens should have a crucial role to play in promoting good governance and ensuring transparency, responsiveness and accountability. The need for strengthening participatory democracy and good governance is an issue of contemporary significance all over the world.

Good Governance

An efficient, effective and democratic government is the best guarantor of social justice as well as an orderly society. Similarly, there is also emphasis on the fact that the administrative system has to be country-specific and area-specific, keeping in view not only the institutions of governance and its legal and regulatory mechanisms, but also keeping the market, civil society and cultural values of the people in view. the government would, therefore, have the singular responsibility to create an enabling environment where development programmes get properly implemented and that creative minds do not get stifled or their energies diverted from undertaking new initiatives or enterprises. the principal response of the state, therefore, would be to facilitate, enable, and coordinate through good governance.

Good governance does not occur by chance. It must be demanded by citizens and nourished explicitly and consciously by the nation-state. It is, therefore, necessary that the citizens are allowed to participate freely, openly and fully in the political process. The citizens must have the right to compete for office, form political parties and enjoy fundamental rights and civil liberties. Good governance is accordingly associated with an accountable political leadership and enlightened policy-making coupled with a civil service imbued with professional ethos. the presence of a strong civil society including a free press and independent judiciary are essential for good governance. Good governance helps create an environment in which sustained economic growth becomes achievable and allows the citizens to maximize their returns on investment. Good governance is about the best possible processes that go into the making and implementing 'correct' decisions. Good decision-making processes, and therefore, good governance, share several characteristics, which have a positive effect on various aspects of government.

Objectives of the Seminar

In the above background, the Institute of Indian Culture organised a 2-day National Seminar on 1 and 2 April, 2017, with a view to discussing the problems in ushering in good governance in India and identify the issues affecting good governance so as to raise awareness amongst all stakeholders about the importance of good governance in relation to human rights and development especially of the weaker sections. It was also proposed to discuss examples of good governance practices undertaken by Non-Governmental Organisations (NGOs) in helping the poorer sections of the population and Dalits. The Seminar was supported by the Indian Council of Social Science Research, Government of India, New Delhi.

Presentations

Dr. Scaria Pannackal's chapter deals with the features of good governance and quotes the definitions held out by the international organisations. He, however, insists that morality among the rulers and administrators is the main foundation of the governing process as it instils public confidence and trust in the government. It is only a government with high moral values that can work for the common good, control corruption, establish democratic pluralism and eliminate poverty. The rulers have to have self-discipline, humility and resist arrogance. In the same vein, *Dr. M.K. George* emphasizes that Good Governance is one which serves the interests of every citizen including the *Daridra Narayans* identified by Gandhiji, and can flourish only in the context of democracy, secularism and social justice.

Dr. Laxmikant Dwivedi refers to the various provisions of the Constitution of India and the rulings of the Supreme Court while insisting that the government must operate according to established, consistent legal principles, and not according to the interest of those who happen to be in power at a given time. It is only under such circumstances that one can expect good governance. *Dr. P.M. Kamath* refers to certain factors like frequent elections and the moral code of conduct set out by the Election Commission that come in the way of execution of development works by the Government. He agrees with the proposal made by Prime Minister Narendra Modi that there could be a single election both for the Parliament and State Assemblies so as to reduce the expenditure and allowing the elected representatives to concentrate on their job instead of getting ready for elections at frequent intervals. Dr. Kamath has suggested direct election of members of the Rajya Sabha at the federal level and the Legislative Councils in States by the people. He also favours direct election of Governors to the States. As a final proposition and the efficacy of these measures, he favours switching over to the presidential system of government.

Dr. Vasundhara Mohan contends that the concept of Good Governance is not new and dates back to the days of Kautilya. She explains the concepts of Good Governance as enunciated by Kautilya and juxtaposes these concepts against the governance in India under Jawaharlal Nehru, Atal Behari Vajpayee and Narendra Modi. It has been ages since Kautilya's *Arthashastra* elucidated the importance for and conditions of a good governance. She wonders whether we achieved even a small percentage of Kautilya's prescription; or those of the World Bank and others for that matter. It has also been almost three years since Narendra Modi started emphasizing on and promising good governance. Has anything changed?

Dr. Leela D'Souza refers to the caste politics in Indian elections and the competition among the political parties for cornering votes in the name of caste and religion. She holds that ensuring inclusive growth in India is not easy, given the deep religious, class and caste divide, both in rural as well as urban sections. Quoting Gandhiji, she argues that the focus needs to be on bringing rural India under good governance and including them in economic and social development. She sounds confident that other problems like population increase will be automatically addressed, when economic development takes place, leading to the demand for education and higher education for their children.

While good governance has to benefit all the sections of the society, it should concern more with the oppressed population. This aspect was discussed by some of the scholars. Good governance also allows space for NGOs that strive for the improvement of the lives of the poorer section, especially Dalits and Adivasis.

In the above context, *Dr. John Solomon Gaikwad* discusses at length the issues relating to the tribal population and the steps taken by the various governments from time to time *vis-à-vis* the constitutional provisions that impact the welfare of the tribals. *Mr. Nirmal Dhanasamy*, who has wide experience of working among the tribals, suggests that the government that promises good governance has to keep the culture, traditions, language of the Adivasis before or while permitting corporate houses and others develop the tribal areas. He expresses concern that exploitation of mineral deposits in tribal areas totally upsets the lives of the tribals unless their lifestyles are taken while relocating them from the project areas. He also mentions that the government has to keep in mind the food habits of the tribals while imposing ban on the consumption of meat.

Expressing his anguish over the plight of Dalits in India, *Dr. R.R. Patil* points out that the overview of Dalit situation in India shows the prevalence of their multi-dimensional discrimination and marginalisation of Dalits in the society. It also shows that even after seventy years of Independence the caste-system and caste-based discrimination are practiced against the Dalits and a majority of the Dalits are the victims of caste-based discrimination. It is the responsibility of the state, civil society organisation and conscious-sympathetic citizens of India to protect and prevent Dalits from all forms of discrimination and exploitation. Dr. Patil presents a case study; that of Navsarjan Trust, an NGO functioning in Gujarat since the early seventies. He narrates in detail the steps taken and being implemented by the Trust in the emancipation of the Dalits by raising the conscience of the community to fight social and economic exploitation. The educational programmes run by the Trust have led the community to assert its rights over surplus lands and question the unequal and unjust social relationship. In the absence of authentic data, Dr. Patil suggests that a comparative study should be undertaken to understand the role and impact of Governmental and Non-Governmental vocational educational institutes in the economic empowerment of Dalits in India.

Dr. Ravindra Singh's chapter discusses the role of Civil Society Organisations (CSO) in ensuring good governance. Dr. Singh also highlights the role of CSO in ensuring greater accountability and transparency and explores the contribution made by CSOs in various roles such as being a watchdog, an advocate, an educator, agitator, service provider etc.

Dr. Prashant Bansode observes that the problem of the Dalit and Adivasi landless agricultural labourers is grave in India. The problem is not only about landlessness, but also concerns the treatment meted out to them as labourers in the feudal set up of the agrarian society in India. He refers to studies that have found that some of the traditional practices of exploitation still continue to persist under which services are taken from the labourers treating them as serfs. Apart from the fact that the traditional system of caste-based services continues to this day, the system of bonded labour in new forms and under new terminologies perpetuates. He argues that if the conditions of the labourers have to improve, land rights are essential for the weaker sections so that they can lead a dignified life and escape discrimination in the agrarian society.

Shifting the focus to yet another weaker sections of the Indian society, *Dr. Vibhuti Patel* observes that one of the basic features of Good Governance should be women's empowerment and creating conditions for gender equality. She insists that no government can claim to be working in the best interests of its population, if it ignores women. She agrees that there are a number of proclaimed women-friendly policies. But, Dr. Patel feels sad that they fail in the implementation of such proclaimed policies. Her chapter discusses gender budgeting by all departments of the government so as to ensure that women form a part and parcel of every government scheme. She also insists that there should be proper monitoring and supervision of the allocated funds for women's welfare with greater transparency and accountability at all levels.

An obvious fan of Narendra Modi, *Dr. Manisha Madhava* presents Modi's style of leadership taking demonetisation as a case study. Apart from the reasons as to why Modi resorted to demonetisation of the Rs. 500 and Rs. 1000 notes, she applauds the way he announced his decision. She points out that the interesting aspect of Modi's leadership style is his use of the media; especially the social media. She states that the fact that Narendra Modi is an inspirational leader was evident during the election campaign, through his political slogans and campaign strategy. Narendra Modi's style of leadership has led to fast and effective decision-making, though it may be lacking the power of collective wisdom. Though he becomes solely responsible for his decisions, the success or failure of the decision is borne by him. According to Dr. Manisha Madhava, Modi has not yet faced any major reverses and has for most part received accolades. While transformative decisions are leadership driven, they have to be strategically implemented and executed and in this task Modi's methodical approach and frontal leadership are clearly evident. She, however, expresses her concern that while these are valuable traits in a leader, these very traits can create the way for authoritarianism, especially if there are little or no institutional checks. The challenge for Narendra Modi lies in providing a strong leadership that the nation yearns without either jeopardizing the institutional backbone or democratic fabric.

Ms. Arpita Shah's chapter deals with the influence of Raychandbhai on Mahatma Gandhi. Wedded to truth and *Ahimsa*, Gandhiji gave importance to ethics. Arpita Shah says that ethic constitute the centrality of a political leader, but it is quite an achievement for a politician of this day and age to abide by the virtues astutely and strictly, without any favour or ill-will towards anyone. In the same vein, ethics form the cornerstone of Good Governance. An ethical society, a society that is grounded in morality and virtues, that puts a premium over spiritual and moral health of its citizens, resolves problems of discord and disharmony in a way that is more evolved and welfare-enhancing. Since the State is composed of a multitude of stake holders, an ethical State would include all of them in its ambit.

1
Features of Good Governance

Scaria Pannackal

Introduction

Governance is essentially the process of decision making and the manner in which the decisions are implemented. Good governance implies a high level of organisational effectiveness in policy formulation and the capacity to implement it. Good governance also implies accountability, transparency, participation, openness and the rule of law.

It is widely believed that poor governance is the main reason for holding back a country's development and progress. How to fix governance and provide people-friendly and responsive public administration is the single biggest challenge before the nations. Numerous high level committees and commissions have given laudable recommendations to reform governance, but they have remained unimplemented and we continue to be trapped in an outdated, dysfunctional, bureaucratic machine. I believe that a lack of ethical and moral compass on the part of our rulers and policy makers is the main reason for all the ills. They are caught in worship of the 'self', forgetting that 'selfless service' is the foundation on which the edifice of public administration rests.

United Nations Development Programme

According to United Nations Development Programme (UNDP), governance not only encompasses the state, but transcends it and includes Private Sector and Civil Society Organisations. UNDP defines governance as the exercise of economic, political and administrative authority to manage a country's affairs at all levels. It comprises the mechanisms, processes and institutions through which citizens and groups articulate their interests, exercise their legal rights, meet their obligations and mediate their differences.[1] Each domain of governance—state, private sector and civil society— has strengths and weaknesses, but the pursuit of good governance requires greater interaction among them to define the right balance for sustainable, people–centred development. The goal of governance initiatives should be to develop capacities that are needed to realise development that gives priority to the poor, advance women, sustains the environment and creates needed opportunities for employment and other forms of livelihood.

UNDP enumerates the following characteristics of governance:

(a) *Participation:* All men and women should have a voice in decision-making either directly or through legitimate intermediate institutions that represent their interests;
(b) *Rule of Law:* Legal frameworks should be fair and enforced impartially;
(c) *Transparency:* It is built on the free flow of information;
(d) *Responsiveness:* Institutions and processes try to serve all stakeholders;
(e) *Consensus Orientation:* Good Governance mediates differing interests to reach a broad consensus on what is in the best interest of the group;
(f) *Equity:* All men and women have opportunities to improve or maintain their well-being;
(g) *Accountability:* Decision-makers in the government, the Private Sector and Civil Society Organisations are accountable to the public as well as to the institutional state holders; and
(h) *Leaders and the Public* have a broad and long term perspective on good governance and human development along with a sense of what is needed for such development.

Commission on Global Governance

The Commission observes that changes in the last half a century have brought the concept of global neighbourhood, a world in which citizens are increasingly dependent on one another and need to co-operate nearer to reality. It calls for a global ethic, a common commitment to core-values that all humanity could uphold: respect for life, liberty, justice, equality, mutual respect, caring and integrity. It prescribes a set of common rights and responsibilities :

(a) It should encompass the right of people to a secure life, equitable treatment, an opportunity to earn a fair living and provide their own welfare, preservation of their own differences through peaceful means, participation in governance at all levels, free and fair petition for redress of gross injustice, equal access to information.

(b) All people should share a responsibility to contribute to the common good, consider the impact of their actions on the security and welfare of others, promote equity including gender equity, protect the interests of future generations by pursuing sustainable development, preserve humanity's cultures and intellectual heritage, be active participants in governance and work to eliminate corruption.

Planning Commission

According to the Planning Commission of India, Good Governance requires efficient institutions, good delivery mechanism and supportive legislation, rules and procedures. The Eleventh Five Year Plan (2007–2012) says that Good governance should cover the following dimensions[2]:

- Constitutionally protected right to elect government at various levels in a fair manner;
- The government must be effective and efficient in delivering social and economic public services;
- Rule of law must be firmly established; and
- The system should function in a fair and inclusive manner.

The Philosophy of New Public Management

The New Public Management Paradigm emphasizes—

(a) that public managers must give high quality services that citizens value;

(b) advocates increased autonomy and reduction of central agency control;
(c) demands managers to meet performance targets; and
(d) emphasizes competition to improve efficiency and rewards organisational and individual performance.

Public Accountability

Public accountability is the most important component of good governance. In a democracy citizens have the right to know what actions have been taken in their name and they should have the means to force corrective actions when government acts in unjust, unethical or illegal manner. Mark Bovens defines accountability as "a social relationship in which an actor feels an obligation to explain and to justify his or her conduct to some significant other".[3] The three important functions of public accountability are:

- Democratic Control;
- Ensuring integrity of governmental operations. There should be safeguards against corruption, nepotism, abuse of power and other forms of unacceptable behaviour; and
- Improvement in performance.

Ethical Commitment for Good Governance

Public personalities can provide good governance only if they have moral and ethical commitment. Public administration is about caring for every citizen and transcends family, ethnicity, gender, racial and religious affiliations. It concerns fostering efficiency, effectiveness and equitable organizations and promoting civic virtues. The resources, at any moment are finite and so we need to marshal those resources wisely to maximise the benefits for all. Ethics lays the foundation for high performance and excellence as the centre of public administration. High integrity and ethics builds legitimacy for political order. Finally, ethical public administrators build community and social capital for a regime.[4] In the words of Yehezkel Dror, "Governance should engage in moral education, facilitating pluralistic ethical notions of a good life, individually and collectively, within a pan-human context."[5]

Corruption in the government is one of the most serious problems across the world. In democracies, electoral competition is becoming increasingly costly for political parties and candidates, forcing them to resort to dishonesty and corruption. Cut-throat competition pushes business owners to look for every advantage including bribing officials when it serves their interest. Mafia, drug traders and criminals combine large bribes with physical intimidation, often placing the governance staff under intolerable pressure. Weakness in social values reinforces vices in governance making public life increasingly immoral. Corruption among senior politicians is one of the most serious pathologies of contemporary governance. Therefore, there is a need to transform the current culture so that the ideals of virtue and character become imperative for senior-politicians and governance elites. The journey to evil is made in small steps not in giant leaps. Evil begins at 15 volts, not 450 volts. No single step embodies evil, but the further down the path you go the harder it is to turn back.[6] The only way of countering wickedness is to operate from a high moral ground and invoke the invisible but strong inner power of moral force. the clash between right and wrong, truth and falsehood is as old as civilization. However, history is a testimony to the fact that it is righteousness that wins ultimately.

The position one holds must be used for the good of the society, for a large cause and not for personal and private gain. When we internalise this stand it becomes difficult to compromise with core values that sustain us. As Pandit Jawaharlal Nehru said "we must act with courage and dignity and stick to the ideals that give meaning to life. Life is empty, if we lose sight of the larger picture and the meaning and purpose of living. When it comes to the question of upholding the principles and values we must see that we do not quit, but stick to the fight."

Good Governance is a Moral Enterprise

Morality provides the main foundation of the governing process as it instils public confidence and trust in the government. Moral governance reflects basic values such as common good, democratic pluralism, controlling corruption etc., where elites dedicate their lives to public service. Good governance also requires conscientious attempts to eliminate poverty, sustaining livelihoods and fulfilling basic needs. Morality can lead to mastery over base characteristics such as greed, exploitation, abuse of power and mistreatment of people. Morality requires self-discipline, humility and resists the arrogance that can come with holding a public office.

According to Caiden and Dwivedi, the objective of good governance is to create an environment in which public servants as well as politicians are able to respond to the challenge of good governance. The challenge for public officials involves a notion of duty as well as acting morally and accountably. If these two dimensions can be brought together in public sector management, it may be possible for public servants to rise above self-interest by placing collective good above private interest and greed. Bringing moral and procedural domains together provides a strong fight against corruption, mismanagement and bad governance. No society, no matter its political and religious orientation can live in spiritual and moral vacuum.[7] Thus, Good governance is essentially a moral enterprise. When power becomes humanly-oriented it becomes spiritual and the man and woman who handles such power becomes a spiritual person with a socially-oriented will.

Values and Ethics: the Concept

If public servants are to fulfil the responsibilities entrusted to them, they must have the right value system. Values are the accepted principles or standards of an individual or a group. The value system we acquire and develop affects our attitudes, preferences, goals and aspirations. It sets standards and guidelines which govern our behaviour, the quality of relationships we build and the responses we make to life situations. Values are like an anchor in a ship. When a storm comes, a ship is not swept away by strong currents, but remains anchored to the shore. A person with strong values or character sticks to his principles and is not swept away, in crisis or under pressure. Ethics is the study of moral standard, and how they affect conduct. Moral is relating to issues of right or wrong and to how individuals should behave. Therefore, morality means standards of conduct that are accepted as right or proper. Character is an asset of qualities that makes a person distinctive, especially qualities of mind and feeling. Character is that ensemble of actualised qualities of head and heart of an individual through the help of which he masters feats and forces of life in a creative manner and gradually reaches self-fulfilment in a way helpful to others. If a man of character is the hope, solace, well-being, peace and inspiration of mankind, a man without character causes trouble, strife, worry, and misery in society. Conduct is the way a person behaves especially in public. Character expresses itself as conduct, which is an outer expression of one's personality.

In the ultimate analysis, moral law is supreme. We also experience that divine intervention comes to our rescue when we do not deviate and have the courage to persist with the chosen right path. In the long chequered history and culture of India we had numerous instances where the wickeds were crushed by the power of a higher moral force and truth. We should not make any mistake in understanding the power of a higher moral force and the truth. Life is a great levelling process and we are here to learn. To learn that pleasure, money, possessions and positions have only limited value. None of these pursuits should be the focal point of our lives. Lessons of fair-play, unselfishness, humility, faithfulness, honesty and truthfulness are important and we must pass on to others.

Principles of Public Service Ethics

Public service is a public trust. Citizens expect public servants to serve the public interest with fairness and to manage public resources properly. Public service ethics are a prerequisite to and are a keystone of good governance. The key principles of public service ethics are:

- Public office being a trust, shall be used only to advance public interests and not personal gains;
- Decisions should be made on merits, free from partiality and prejudice;
- Discharge government policies/decisions openly, efficiently, equitably and honourably so that the public can make informed judgement and hold public officials accountable;
- Honour and respect democratic principle; and
- Safeguarded public confidence in the integrity of government by avoiding impropriety and conduct unbefitting a public official.

The Missing Ethical Environment

Today, we are facing a crisis of values which is reflected in lack of concern for fellow human beings, a culture of greed and widespread corruption which afflicts every facet of life. Swami Ranganathananda says that many people holding power and authority are spiritually weak and therefore, indulge in violence, selfishness and corruption.[8] When a person combines power with spiritual inwardness, authority with sensitiveness to ethical and human values and social responsibilities, that person becomes a true public servant; work efficiency should be combined with ethical and moral efficiency.

Ethics cannot be shaped and sustained in isolation; it requires supportive environment—both political and social. It is the primary responsibility, of the state to promote an environment which supports high standard of conduct and moral values in society. This needs an all-encompassing approach, by imparting right kind of education to the children and youth in schools and colleges, by ensuring ethical conduct of persons working in public services including politicians and by creating an environment of honesty and trust for business and industry to thrive. The Vice President of India, Hamid Ansari expressed concern that the legal and administrative steps taken so far to improve ethical norms in the executive, the legislature and the judiciary are inadequate and called for more purposeful, result-oriented approach.[9]

The public services must set the example of high standard of conduct and ethical behaviour if the country is to make progress and develop. For this it is necessary that the state creates a suitable ethics infrastructure for public services to flourish and thrive. Most developed countries that are rated high on good governance index have created effective ethics infrastructure, inducing a code of Values and Ethics for public servants, from which we can draw valuable lessons.

Our primitive loyalties based on religion, caste and language come in direct conflict with our loyalty to the nation. Then we become communal, divide people and spread hatred and violence in the name of religion and language. We need to rise above this parochial and chauvinistic mind-set. We need to think big. We should not fall prey to politicians who use religion, caste and language to divide us and build their political base. If the environment in which we live is charged with hatred and mutual distrust, we cannot feel safe and secure. We must respect the diversity and learn to tolerate the differences and live in communal harmony—the essence of Indian ethos.

The need for ethical and moral values for regeneration of society is hardly a new or revolutionary idea. I am convinced that reinstatement of values and ethics in public life will help us fight corruption and other evils afflicting Society. Currently, the world, especially our country, is passing through a difficult time and the national mood is one of disappointment, frustration and pessimism. But we should not become cynical and give up. Great men who have made a difference to this world tell us that we should work tirelessly for a good and noble cause, however, difficult the task is. The government that we have is our own making. It is not imposed on us by any alien power. It is within us to improve the quality of governance and the public life and to make the politicians and the public functionaries responsible and accountable. Corruption, communal divide and terrorism plaguing our country are the manifestations of our own failings as a people. One of the main reasons for the rise in crime and communal violence is denial of justice. When system is not just and fair in rewarding and punishing people, it breeds corruption, crime and violence. We need to do something to change the system, rather than complaining all the time and doing nothing.

Conclusion

Public administration is a value driven activity with deep moral grounding and unless the holders of public office, particularly the ministers and senior members of civil services, observe high moral standards and imbibe core values of integrity and objectivity, the administration cannot serve the interests of people. today the ruling elite lacks the character and discipline needed to govern impartially and firmly. Unless we destroy corruption in high places, root out every trace of nepotism, love of power, profiteering and black marketing which have spoiled the good name of countries in recent times we will not be able to raise the standards of efficiency of administration. "In the happiness of his subjects lies the king's happiness; in their welfare his welfare. He shall not consider as good only that which pleases him, but treat as beneficial to him whatever pleases his subject".[10]

Notes

1. Agarwal, P.K., and N. Vittal (2005) *I am Sorry: Indian Bureaucracy at Crossroads*, Delhi: Manas Publications.

2. Ansari, M. Hamid and V.N. Tewari, Lecture on *Private Ethics and Public Morality*, Punjab University, Chandigarh, 10 April, 2010.
3. Arora, Hari C. (1996) "Indian Administrative Culture and Bureaucracy", in T.N. Chaturvedi (Ed.) *Contemporary Administrative Culture in India,* New Delhi : Indian Institute of Public Administration.
4. Bovens, Mark (2005) "Public Accountability", in E. Ferlie, L. Lynn and C. Pollit (Eds.) *The Oxford Handbook of Public Management*, Oxford University Press.
5. Caiden, Gerald E. (2001) "Corruption and Democracy", in Gerald E. Caiden, O.P. Dwivedi and Joseph Jabbra (Eds.) *Where Corruption Lives*, West Hartford : Kumarian Press.
6. Commission on Global Governance, Our Global Neighbourhood, *A Report of the Commission on Global Governance*, New York : Oxford University Press (1995).
7. Das, Gurcharan (2009) *The Difficulty of Being Good*, New Delhi : Allen Lane.
8. Gandhi, M.K., (2011) *India of My Dreams,* Ahmedabad : Navajivan Publishing House.
9. Gill, S.S. (2000) The *Pathology of Corruption*, New Delhi : Harper Collins.
10. Jonathan, Boston (2001) Andrew Bradstock and David Eng. (Ed.) *Ethics and Public Policy: Contemporary Issues*, Wellington NZ : Victoria University Press.

References

Khanna, Justice H.R. (1998) "Ethics in Public Life: Issues and Remedy", in Raj K. Nigam (Ed.) *Public Accountability in Indian Polity*, New Delhi: D.C. Publications.

Hota, P.C. (2006) "Excellence in Public Service", in *Indian Journal of Public Administration*, Special Number, Vol. 52, No. 3, July-September, pp. 322-40.

Kangle, R.P. (1997) Kautilya's *Arthashastra,* Delhi : Motilal Banarsidass.

Michael Shermer (2015) *The Moral Arc*, New York : Henry Holt & Company.

Ramachandram, G. (2017) *The Trial by Fire*, Wordizen Books.

Tripathi, A.N. (2009) *Human Values*, New Delhi : New Age International.

2

De-Constructing the Tripod of Good Governance

Democracy, Secularism and Social Justice

M.K. George S.J.

Introduction

Good governance has become the dream and buzzword in the minds of every citizen. Faced with abominable levels of corruption and unable to make any creative intervention in spite of all the assurances of the state and non-state actors, there is a sustained hope in the minds of every citizen that good governance can be the one significant move towards realising the Constitutional dream of social justice. Good governance, understood as serving the interests of every citizen including the *Daridra Narayans* identified by Gandhiji, can flourish only in the context of democracy, secularism and social justice. Hence, the usage tripod of good governance makes sense.

Unfortunately, over the years, particularly since the 1990s when a globalised economy in India radically changed the discourse on socio-economic and political reality, there is a marked de-construction of the very terms Good Governance, Secularism and Social Justice. There is almost a total negation of these concepts or reversal of understanding.

This Chapter tries to look at this radical de-construction of the terms and its impact in practice. The argument is that concepts matter and definitions determine the course of action. Good governance will happen only when we also attend to the conceptual; a role definitely assigned to the intellectual community.

De-Construction as an Everyday Exercise

De-construction is defined as "the analytic examination of something (as a theory) often in order to reveal its inadequacy". *Deconstruction* does not actually mean "demolition"; instead it means "breaking down" or analysing something (especially the words in a work of fiction or non-fiction) to discover its true significance, which is supposedly, almost never exactly, what the author intended. "A feminist may *deconstruct* an old novel to show how even an innocent-seeming story somehow depends on the oppression of women. A new Western may deconstruct the myths of the old West and show lawmen as vicious and criminals, as flawed but decent. Table manners, the *Sound of Music,* and cosmetics advertirements have all been the subjects of *deconstructionist* analysis. Of course, not everyone agrees with deconstructionist interpretations, and some people reject the whole idea of deconstruction, but most of us have run into it by now even if we did not realise it." (Merriam-Webster)

In this sense, de-construction of concepts, assumptions and theories happen continuously as a process. It is happening in the intellectual discourses, political arguments and even in everyday discourse of the lay people. We do not notice its everydayness, but only feel it when suddenly we realise that the meanings have changed from what we have been used to. Let us look at this process with reference to the concepts we are discussing now: Good Governance, Democracy, Secularism and Social Justice. While it may be ambitious to do this within the limits of a short paper, I would like to do it in broad strokes and comparing two periods of Indian history: Post-Independent and Post-Globalized (since 1990s).

Good Governance

We are used to looking at good governance as a process of achieving justice for all and the good of all. But, there is a different take on it too. For instance, "Governance refers to the institutions and relations to do with political power: the way political power is exercised and legitimised. In other words, governance is constructed primarily on the terrain of power. Thus articulated, the values and principles by which governance would be judged and characterised relate to forms of governance, such as democratic governance, authoritarian governance or dictatorial governance. The "Good governance" discourse, however, does not consider the relationships of power. Rather, it presents itself as a *moral* paradigm, distinguishing between the good, the bad and the evil. What is 'good' and 'bad' governance thus turns out to be a moral judgement on the one hand, and relativist and subjectivist on the other. The result is that 'good governance' has no conceptual or theoretical value in understanding the phenomenon with a view to changing it. Rather it is, at best, a propagandist tool, easily manipulatable by whoever happens to wield power. And this is exactly how it has been deployed in the dominant, neo-liberal discourse (Issa G. Shivaji, 2003).

Democracy

Similarly, understanding of democracy is changing all over the world too. "Liberal democracy, which is fundamentally different from electoral or populist democracy, is in apparent decline around the globe in quality and, worryingly, in popular acceptability. Now, its shakiness in the US has been noted by a couple of respected watchdog institutions" (Adhikari, 2017).

How democratic is India after seven decades of political independence? There are two voices, the optimist and the pessimist. 'India remains the world's largest democracy at a time when large parts of the world are entering an age of uncertainty. If it can make democracy function better, and produce governance that is responsive, it will provide a bulwark and an example against the global forces of instability...the nub of frustration with politics, whether at the local or national level, is usually over the failure of good governance and the implementation of policies" (French, 2016).

On the other side, we see the progressive deterioration of democratic institutions. "Strength and quality of a democratic polity, in a large measure, depends on the functioning of the constitutional institutions—Parliament, the Executive and the Judiciary. Over the last 70 years since Independence, these have declined in their effectiveness and prestige" (Dua, 2017).

Comparing the institutions of democracy as the Immune System of a Society, Anand (2017) says that the various estates are the government, parliament, judiciary, and the fourth estate, the Media. Added to these, there is a fifth estate, the Civil Society. Anand points out the fast deterioration in all these institutional arrangements. The Government has become riddled with corruption and slow response to the needs of the people. "In India much of the corruption is strongly associated with the bureaucracy, command organisations, public sector and other contributional and statutory bodies" (Valerian Rodrigues, 2017); the Parliament has become almost non-functional for years, with neither the ruling party nor the opposition parties keen on an effective functioning; the judiciary, he says, has become like a post office clerk, stamping everything in front of them. The fourth estate has become subservient to the vested interests of those in power. The intellectuals are afraid to write. They re-write, stop writing and burn what they have written. Fear grips everyone. Speaking in a similar vein, Sasikumar (2017) wrote that media has become slave to the ratings and advertisements. If there is no rating, there is no advertisement. Hence, it becomes a mad race for ratings and advertisements. In the aftermath, truth suffers. We do not have mechanisms to read reality beyond what the political *pandits* and media give.

The Role of Civil Society

A strong civil society can ensure the success of good governance. However, it is good to assess the situation of the Civil Society Organisations in the country today. There has been a widespread crackdown on Civil Society Organisations in the pretext of financial irregularities, terrorism etc. Quite a few whistle-blowers have been killed and their killers have not even been identified. Writers have stopped writing or withdrawn publication. Thus, overall there is a fear created in the minds of Civil Society Actors which is, once again, a very threatening factor for democracy.

Shiv Visvanath (2016) wrote: "Democracy in India becomes caught between two straitjacket solutions, each of which adds to the problem. We are caught between an impoverished secularism and an overwrought communalism. Each acts with a piety and righteousness which makes deliberation different. When belief is tied to electoral votes, rational decision making becomes difficult. The logic of electoralism makes secular thought uneasy, allowing it to teeter to one minoritarian edge or the other. Secularism also tends to be aridly statist and uniform, emptying India of the sheer diversity and plurality of its imagination. In a biographical sense, it is often a young mass belief. Secularists like Nehru or Chandra Shekhar had their ashes sprinkled on the Ganges, affirming at least a "cosmic solidarity". And that leads us to Secularism.

Secularism

"When the founding fathers made secularism a basic feature of the Constitution, it was expected that this would become a cementing force among all religious communities. However, experience over the last 70 years has shown that secularism has become a bone of contention among all communities. It is difficult to believe that none of the communities are satisfied with the manner in which secularism has been practised. While Hindus believe that minority communities are being unduly appeased as vote banks, minority communities feel that injustice has been done to them in all matters of development and their welfare" (Madhav Godbole, 2016).

Commenting on the recent political events in India, Arti R. Jerath (2017) wrote, "in recent times more worrying is the decimation of secularism as a foundational political philosophy". Post-Independence, we noticed an interpretation of secularism which respected every religion and kept distance from every religion. However, over the years, electoral politics made every party play with diluting the concept and eventually we have reached a stage very well put by an observer. "From the notorious **Shah Bano case** in the 1980s to the promotion of stereotyped meat-trader-musclemen candidates in 2017, nothing has been more damaging to the cause of secularism than repeated cynical manipulation of the Muslim vote by avowedly secular leaders themselves...". Now, we have reached a stage where "a saffron-clad monk holding political office..." (Nalin Mehta, 2017). Pseudo-secularism dominates the political discourse today and the value of secularism *per se* has been lost. So, where do we go from here?

Social Justice

Discourses have changed focus from social justice to Development. It is arguments for development, GDP, growth rate and statistics-based arguments for development that fill the current atmosphere. The theory that dominates the thinking of all seems to be "Trickledown theory of development". And most Indian citizens, at least if we go by the voting patterns, seem to believe that what matters now is only development, little realising that development is not a value-neutral concept nor is it by its own nature assurance of social justice.

Let us look at some of the data on the effect of development. Rated as the seventh largest economy in the world and recently overtaking even Britain in its economic growth, where do we stand in terms of distribution and social justice? "According to a report by the Johannesburg-based company New World Wealth, India is the second-most unequal country globally, with millionaires controlling 54 per cent of its wealth. With a total individual wealth of $ 5600 billion, it is among the 10 richest countries in the world; and yet the average Indian is relatively poor. Compare this with Japan, the most equal country in the world, where according to the report millionaires control only 22 per cent of its total wealth. In India, the richest 1 per cent own 53 per cent of the country's wealth. The richest 5 per cent own 68.6 per cent while the top 10 per cent have 76.3 per cent. At the other end of the pyramid, the poorer half jostles for a mere 4.1 per cent of national wealth.

Oxfam (2016) believes that this sharp rise in inequality in India —and in many countries around the world—is damaging, and that countries need to make an effort to curb it. Rising inequality will lead to slower poverty reduction, undermines the sustainability of economic growth, and compounds the inequalities between men and women and drive inequalities in health, education and life chances."

Post-Truth Society

What makes the discourses on good governance, democracy, secularism and social justices more difficult and confusing is the fact that we have moved into a post-truth society. for those of us who still may not be familiar with the concept, here is a brief introduction. After much discussion, debate, and research, the *Oxford Dictionary Word* of the Year 2016 is *post-truth;* an adjective defined as "relating to or denoting circumstances in which objective facts are less influential in shaping public opinion than appeals to emotion and personal belief."

"Two key events of 2016 shaped our understanding of the post-truth world: one was in June, when Britain voted in favour of leaving the European Union. the other was in November, when political maverick Donald Trump was elected the 45th President of the United States of America. Trump's administration spent the third day of his Presidency speaking of "alternative facts", and making false claims about the size of the crowds that had attended his inauguration."

"Wake up and smell the post-truth", says an observer. India is home of post-truth politics, says Ranjit Goswami. From education to health care and the economy, particularly its slavish obsession with GDP, India can be considered a world leader in post-truth politics. India's post-truth era cannot be traced to a single year—its complexities go back to generations. But the election in 2014 can be marked as a significant inflection point. Ever since, the country has existed under majoritarian rule with widely reported discrimination against minorities.

India's version of post-truth is different to its Western counterparts due to the country's socio-economic status; its per capita nominal income is less than 3 per cent of that of the US (or 4% of that of the UK). Still, post-truth is everywhere in India. It can be seen in our booming Wall Street but failing main streets; our teacher-less schools and our infrastructure-less villages. We have the ability to influence the world without enjoying good governance or basic living conditions for so many at home. Our government has shown how key decisions can be completely divorced from the everyday lives of Indian citizens, but spun to seem like they have been made for their benefit. Nowhere is this more evident than with India's latest demonetisation drive, which plunged the country into crisis, against the advice of its central bank, and hit poorest people the hardest.

Despite the levels of extreme poverty in India, when it comes to social development, the cult of growth dominates over the development agenda; a trend that it has exacerbated, but that started with past governments. In any democratic society, the pendulum of public opinion swings from one pole to another. In the US and the UK, as in India, we are now seeing the pendulum swing to a populist or post-truth extreme (http://theconversation.com/india-has-been-a-post-truth-society-for-years-and-maybe-the-west-has-too-71169).

In a post-truth society, our own discussions become confusing and dense. Then imagine the confusion added by the whole de-construction of the concepts. What should be the role of the academics today? It looks to me that it should be to keep the discourse going. Face the fear that has gripped the civil society groups. Populism is currently governing the world. Can the academics help create an environment where in meaningful discourses challenge the de-construction processes and achieve certain amount of equanimity in understanding.

Conclusion

The post-truth society that we are in demands alertness. Eternal vigilance is the price we pay for freedom. As Paul Krugmanthe, Nobel Laureate for economic science, recently wrote in his blog, "for things to change, enough people will have to take a stand. Playing it safe is betraying not only your country, but also humankind." the Academic community particularly has this responsibility to keep the conversations going, allow differing opinions to dialogue and arrive at consensuses which will benefit everyone, especially the most marginalised.

References

Mujawwar, W.R. and N.K. Sardar (2012) *Democracy, Good Governance and Human Rights*, Delhi : Neha Publishers and Distributors.

Sasikumar (2017) "Weeping truths and the need for self-selection" (Malayalam – *Vilapichunilkunna Sathyangalum swayamnadathenda thiranjeduppum). Mathrubhumi* weekly March 5-11.

French, Patrick (2016), In the *Week*. December, pp. 66-68.

Jerath, Arti R. (2017) "Modi wave defines election" in *Times of India*. March 13, p. 8.

Dua, H.K. (2016) Space for democracy is shrinking, in the *Week*, December 25.

Adhikari, Gautam (2017) As the World Spins, *Times of India*, 18 February.

Goswami, Ranjit (2017) India has been a Post-Truth Society for years. (Available at http://theconversation.com/india-has-been-a-post-truth-society-for-years-and-maybe-the-west-has-too-71169

Shivaji, Issa G., *Good Governance, Bad Governance and the quest for democracy in Africa: An Alternative Perspective*. A Plenary Lecture presented to Nordic Africa Days, held in Uppsala, Sweden from October 3 to 5, 2003, (Available at http://hakielimu.org/files/publications/document67good_bad_governance_en.pdf)

3

Good Governance, Rule of Law and the Right to Health

Laxmikant Dwivedi

Introduction

The aphorism, "every nation gets the government it deserves", may or may not be true, but there is not an iota of doubt that the happiness of society is the end of a government.

The traditional notion of government and the contemporary notion of governance both are associated with the act of governing. It is in effect the process of decision making and decision implementing. These decisions are meant to regulate the interaction of the members of the society. The larger objective being of establishing a social equilibrium so is to enable each member of the society to attain his or her full potential as a human being and also to realise the social aspirations and goals.

Good Governance is Both a Journey and a Destination

In the Indian context the directive principles of state policy indicate the road map for the destination of good governance. Article 12 of the Constitution of India provides for an inclusive definition State as including "the Government and the Parliament of India and the Government and the Legislature of each of the states....", wherein the significance of State lies in the fact that the State is placed with responsibilities, duties, obligations to ensure the constitutional protection of the individual's rights and entitlements against the State.[1]

In *S.R. Bommai* vs. *Union of India*, the Supreme Court observed: "the Indian Constitution is both a legal and social document. It provides machinery for the governance of the country. It also contains the ideals expected by the nation. The political machinery created by the Constitution is a means to the achieving of this ideal."[2]

The doctrine of government of laws implies that the government must operate according to established, consistent legal principles, and not according to the interest of those who happen to be in power at a given time.[3] Good governance and the rule of law are closely associated with each other, as the rule of law is the most civilised conception of a state and state foundations cannot be built without the rule of law. The attributes of the doctrine of rule of law by Dicey in the Indian context are contained in Part III of the Constitution, which functions as the regulator on the law making power of the parliament.

Constitutional equality is inherent in the rule of law which has been incorporated by the framers in the Right to Equality enshrined in Articles 14-18 and Right to freedoms, life and liberty enshrined in Articles 19-22 of the Constitution of India. Rule of law ensures supremacy of regular power as opposed to arbitrary power and further that every person is subject to the ordinary law within the jurisdiction.

The Supreme Court in *Bachan Singh* vs. *State of Punjab* stated that the rule of law excludes arbitrariness and unreasonableness. The Court said that to ensure rule of law it is necessary for the government to be democratic in making laws and further that there should be an independent judiciary to limit the powers of the legislature and the executive.[4] The judgement in *A.D.M. Jabalpur* vs. *Shivkant Shukla* reiterated the two essential principles of rule of law. the Court said: " ... rule of law is the antithesis of arbitrariness .... Rule of law is now the accepted norm of all the civilised societies.... Everywhere it is identified with the liberty of the individual. It seeks to maintain a balance between the opposing notion of individual liberty and public order."[5]

Rule of law ensures supremacy of regular power as opposed to arbitrary power, and further that every person is subject to the ordinary law within the jurisdiction.[6] It is said that the rule of law must run closely with the rule of life.

In the famous words of Justice Field of the USA Supreme Court, "By the term life, as here used, something more is meant than mere animal existence. The inhibition against its deprivation extends to all those limbs and faculties by which life is enjoyed."[7]

In a recent study[8] using a novel Rule of Law index based on eight sub-indices concluded that a country's adherence to the rule of law is a foundational determinant of health and has suggested that health advocates should consider the improvement of rule of law as a tool to improve the health of the people.

As per the Constitution of the World Health Organization, 'health' " is a state of complete physical, mental and social well-being and not merely the absence of disease or infirmity." The WHO Constitution further incorporates "the enjoyment of the highest attainable standard of health is one of the fundamental rights of every human being without distinction of race, religion, and political belief, economic or social conditions. Thus, all human beings have a right to highest attainable standards of health. Similarly, Article 12 of the International Covenant on Economic, Social and Cultural Rights, 1996 mandates State Parties to take steps to achieve full realisation of the right of everyone to the enjoyment of the highest attainable standard of physical and mental health by the creation of conditions which would assure medical service and medical attention in the event of sickness.

The National Health Mission envisages achievement of universal access to equitable affordable and quality health care services that are accountable to people's needs. The draft National Health Policy 2015 had proposed universal, affordable health care and had projected its intent to make health a fundamental right as a natural corollary of the right to life under Article 21. The WHO has also been advocating universal health care.

The recently formulated National Health Policy 2017 of the present Government notably does not mention about making right to health care as a fundamental right; it does, however, offer the pious hope of "realising health care as a right in future". The policy question regarding making healthcare a fundamental right appears to have been differed for want of basic health infrastructure across the country and the policy advocates "instrumental assurance based approach" for making healthcare as a fundamental right in the future.

Articles 38, 39, 41, 42, 47 and 48A of the Constitution mandate the State to direct its policy to promote and protect the health and welfare of the people.

In 1950, the Union Government enacted the Drugs (Control) Act to control the sale, supply and distribution of drugs. The Drugs and Cosmetics Act was enacted to regulate the import, manufacture, distribution and sale of drugs and cosmetics. In order to stop undesirable advertisements and to save the ignorant and unwary masses, the Drugs and Magic Remedies (Objectionable Advertisements) Act, 1954 was enacted. the Act controls the advertisement of drugs and prohibits advertisement of remedies alleged to possess magic qualities. Similarly, in order to save pregnant women's health and life, the Medical Termination of Pregnancy Bill was introduced in the Parliament in August 1971 and it came on the statute book as the Medical Termination of Pregnancy Act, 1971. Again, with a view to prohibit prenatal diagnostic techniques for determining the gender of the foetus leading to female feticide, a legislation to regulate the use of prenatal diagnostic techniques was enacted by the Parliament as the Preconception and Prenatal Diagnostic Techniques (Prohibition of Sex Selection) Act, 1994. The Transplantation of Human Organs Act, 1994 is a comprehensive legislation to regulate the removal of organs from living as well as deceased persons and transplantation of such organs, and to prohibit commercial dealings in human organs. In the twelfth year of the Republic, The Parliament enacted the Maternity Benefit Act, 1961 to regulate the employment of women before and after child-birth and to provide for payment of maternity benefits to women. The Clinical Establishments Act, 2010 was passed by parliament to regulate clinical standards both in the private health sector and also the public health sector and most importantly to end quackery.

In *Consumer Education and Research Centre & Ors.* vs. *Union of India & Ors,*[9] the Supreme Court observed that the jurisprudence of personhood or the philosophy of the right to life envisaged in Article 21 of the Constitution enlarges its sweep to encompass human personality in its full bloom with invigorated health.

In *Kirloskar Bros Ltd.* vs. *ESI Corporation*, the Supreme Court, while dealing with the application of the ESI Act, enlarged the sphere of obligation to provide health facilities. The Court said, "In expanding economic activity in liberalised economy, Part IV of the Constitution enjoins not only the State and its instrumentalities but even private industries to ensure safety to the workman and to provide facilities and opportunities for health and vigour of the workman assured in relevant provisions and in Part IV which are integral part of right to equality under Article 21 which are fundamental rights to the workman."[10]

The Supreme Court has accorded top priority to public health. In *Vincent Panikurlangara* vs. *Union of India*, the Court observed that "maintenance and improvement of public health have to rank high as these are indispensable to the very physical betterment of these depends the building of society of which the constitution makers envisages. Attending to public health, in our opinion, therefore, is of high priority—perhaps the one at the top."[11]

In *Murli Deora* vs. *Union of India & Ors.*[12] the Supreme Court was dealing with a Public Interest Litigation about banning smoking in public places. The Court after considering the harmful effect that smoking has on non-smokers, prohibited smoking in public. It also issued directions to the governments to take effective steps to ensure prohibiting smoking in all public places.

In *Tapan Kumar Sadhukhan* vs. *Food Corporation of India & Ors*,[13] the Supreme Court stated that the Food Corporation of India (FCI) being an agency of the State, it must conform to the letter and spirit of Article 41 of the Constitution and, as such, the trading activity by the FCI must be done in keeping in view the constitutional obligation to improve public health. The case was about substandard rice being released in market. The Court was concerned about public health being jeopardized, if such substandard rice was to be consumed by members of the public on account of illiteracy, ignorance and poverty, if sold at cheap rates. The Court directed the FCI to upgrade the entire stock of rice and make it suitable for human consumption.

Similarly, in *Swami Achyutanand Tirth's case*,[14] which was a public interest litigation highlighting the menace of sale of adulterated and synthetic milk in various states, the Supreme Court directed the Union Government of India and the State Governments to take appropriate steps to implement the Food Safety and Standards Act, 2006 effectively and to increase consumer awareness about the ill effects of milk adulteration and to educate the general public and school children through workshops and teaching them easy methods for detection of common adulterants in food.

The apathy towards victims of road accidents prompted the Supreme Court in *Parmanad Katara's case*[15] to issue directives to hospitals and doctors reminding them about their obligation to the society and their duty to extend medical assistance in preserving life.

In *Paschim Banga Khet Mazdoor Samiti*,[16] the Supreme Court listed seven specific measures to deal with emergency medical cases. The Court emphasized that it is the Constitutional obligation of the State to provide sufficient medical services to the people at large and lack of financial resources cannot be an excuse. The Supreme Court held, "the Constitution envisages the establishment of a welfare state at the federal level as well as at the state level. In a welfare state the primary duty of the government is to serve the welfare of the people. Providing adequate medical facilities for the people is an essential part of the obligations undertaken by the government in a welfare state. the government discharges the obligation by running hospitals and health centres which provide medical care to the person seeking to avail of those facilities. Article 21 imposes an obligation on the State to safeguard the right to life of every person." The Court highlighted that just as in the context of the constitutional obligation to provide free Legal Aid the State cannot avoid its obligation on account of financial constraints, similarly in the matter of providing medical aid to preserve human life the State cannot plead financial constraints and has to discharge its constitutional obligation.

In *State of Punjab & Ors.* vs. *Ram Lubhaya Bagga*, the Supreme Court addressed the right to health under Article 21 from right-duty perspective. The Court observed, "when we speak about a right, it correlates to a duty upon another, individual, employer, government or authority. In other words, the right of one is an obligation of another. Hence, the right of a citizen to life under Article 21 casts an obligation on the State. This obligation is further reinforced under Article 47; it is for the State to secure health to its citizens as its primary duty.......The State can neither urge nor say that it has no obligation to provide medical facility. If that were so it would be *ex facie* violative of Article 21,"[17] The ground reality in matters of health care is far from the implied constitutional mandate contained in the letter and the spirit of law.

The Maternity Benefit (Amendment) Act, 2017 has enhanced the maternity leave period from 12 to 26 weeks. Many start-ups and small enterprises prefer to hire men over women and substantial number of them believes that the new law would have a negative impact on their cost and profitability.[18] There is disincentive for implementing the new rule as it is the employer who bears the costs alone. The six month maternity break may well prove to be a set back and widen the gender gap in the workforce.

In February 2017, a 26-year old lady died in a nursing home in Sangli (Maharashtra) while undergoing a medical termination of pregnancy, allegedly coerced to undergo the abortion operation by her spouse as the sex determination test revealed that she was carrying a girl. Investigations have revealed of an interstate racket that conducted illegal sex determination tests and abortions for families desperate to have a male child.[19]

In the month of March 2017, it is reported that there have been over half a dozen instances of patients' kith and kin attacking doctors at public hospitals across various districts of Maharashtra including Mumbai.[20] The Maharashtra Medicare Services Persons and Medicare Services Institutions (Prevention of Violence and Damage of Property) Act, 2010 has remained hidden in the statute book as no prosecutions have been initiated under the Act in spite of attacks on doctors and damage to health care facilities.

The Supreme Court recently turned down a woman's plea to medically terminate her 27-week pregnancy with foetal abnormalities as according to the Court the baby could be born alive though with severe physical and mental challenges.[21] While the State gives itself the power to deny a woman the right to abort a foetus, the State does not have any mechanism to support the woman and care for the child. Recently in Mumbai, a toddler who got severe internal injuries was turned away by seven hospitals before breathing his last in Sion Hospital. According to newspaper report, the father of the child, a daily wage worker from Virar, has blamed the hospitals for refusing to admit his son. He said that the hospitals refused a bed to their son, Shahbas, by either saying they were unavailable or demanded a steep admission deposit from them.[22] Again in Bengaluru, a 35-year old stroke patient lost his life while being shunted in an ambulance from one hospital to another.[23] The Chief Minister of Maharashtra has admitted that over 254 children succumbed to malnutrition and 195 foetal deaths have been recorded in Palghar district in the last year.[24]

In view of the foregoing examples, if the adage health is wealth has to have any constitutional relevance, the vision of good governance as contained in Part IV must cease to be mere pious obligation and must translate into affirmative action, else all initiatives, health policy, laws with best of intentions are futile and the constitutional promise contained in Article 21 will always remain an elusive mirage.

References

1. Pradeep Kumar Biswas *v.* Indian Institute of Chemical Biology, (2002) 5 SCC 111.
2. AIR 1994 SC 1918.

3. *Black's Law Dictionary*, Tenth Edition.
4. AIR 1980 SC 898.
5. AIR1976 SC 1207.
6. *Black's Law Dictionary*, Tenth Edition.
7. Munn *v*. Illinois (1876), Page 94 US 113).
8. http://bmjopen.bmj.com/on June 16, 2016. Published by group.bmj.com
9. AIR 1995 SC 922.
10. AIR 1996 SC 3261.
11. AIR 1987 SC 990.
12. (2001) 8 SCC 765.
13. (1996) 6 SCC 101.
14. http://judis.nic.in/supremecourt/imgs1.aspx?filename=43837.
15. AIR 1989 SC 2039.
16. AIR 1996 SC 2426.
17. AIR 1998 SC 1703.
18. *Times of India*, March 24, 2017.
19. *Mumbai Mirror*, March 8, 2017.
20. *Hindustan Times*, March 26, 2017.
21. *Times of India*, March 27, 2017.
22. *DNA*, February 7, 2017.
23. *Deccan Herald*, February 12, 2017.
24. *Hindustan Times*, September 29, 2016.

4

Legal and Constitutional Measures to Drive Good Governance in Practice in Indian Society

P.M. Kamath

Introduction

To begin with, we need to understand what we mean by two popular phrases 'Good Governance' and 'Democracy'. 'Good Governance' begins with mainly the government in power at a given time. But good governance could also be and should also be the goal of all Non-Governmental Organisations (NGOs). In this chapter, our focus is only on Good governance in a government set up by the Constitution and local self-government bodies set up by law.

In a welfare state, the government touches human life from cradle to grave through its governing process—as a liberal, even if you would like to keep the government's interventions in human life to the minimum. Though government's governing process touches everyone's life, it is always seen as bureaucratic, legalistic and without a human touch!

When we need it to be qualified with the adjective 'good', despite being bureaucratic and operating within the legal framework, nothing prevents within a government the governance to be 'good', if only the bureaucrat-in-charge places himself in the shoes of the service seeker, to understand the ordeals faced by a service-seeker from the service provider.

In the 1980s, this author had dealt with the approach of public servants in the US and India. In India 'public' is no concern of the public administrators![1] The service provider will ask an applicant to fulfil deficiencies in his request. But all the deficiencies or requirements will not be made known to the applicant in one visit. But, he will be informed of the lacunae or deficiencies in piecemeal, thus making him pay several visits. It is this attitude that has necessitated Right to Service Act. But a careful analysis will reveal that it helps the bureaucracy to proliferate.[2]

On the other hand, American public servants would go out of the way to help; 'May I help you' is not merely a slogan for them[3] as in India, where the 'May I help you' cubicle is more often empty or provides space for the employees to sleep or have their lunch! A visit to the nearest railway station will prove this point.

Democracy on the other hand, is a form of government which has come into being from the experiences of ruins of all other forms tried by human beings during the historical past. After the end of the Soviet Union in December 1991, which tried one party rule in the name of communism which failed, its successor state, the Russian Federation calls itself democracy. According to Francis Fukuyama, in 1989 Liberal democracy triumphed; with what he called "end of history," "that is, the end point of mankind's ideological evolution and the universalization of western liberal democracy as the final form of human government."[4] Today, democracy has become a dominant form of government, embracing all isms—capitalism, communism, dictatorship, socialism etc. Individual dictatorships also call themselves as guided democracy or basic democracy. Even surviving communist China calls itself as People's democracy!

Democracy, i.e. 'people's power' has several forms all over the world depending upon how deep are its roots in a country. If we take even the West as a region, the differences are so much at variance that it will be a separate book if we begin to comment on it. Yet it is possible to make a beginning by taking a definition offered by Robert M. McIver, long back. He defines democracy as a form of government where people decide 'who will rule' them for a definite period and for 'what purposes'.[5] In all democracies, 'who rules' is decided by periodical elections and for 'what purposes' is decided mostly through the manifesto of winning party or coalition of parties and their campaign promises. This is a minimum requirement for a democracy and we can say that Indian democracy fulfils these criterion.

In comparison to the 1970s, more citizens[6] in India are interested and feel a need to enrich Indian democracy now so that it can deliver 'good governance'. After all, democracy gives the right to expect;

citizens can nourish many hopes to be fulfilled by a government. Periodical elections help citizens as the voters to punish parties which are perceived to have failed to keep their promises. Existence of two political parties or coalitions stands out secure accountability of political parties. American text books for instance state that all politicians might be rascals, but nation needs a set of two to make democracy flourish!

Flaws and Obstructions in Indian Democracy Today

India as an ancient civilisation and culture but as a newly established political democracy with Parliamentary form of government, has fairly worked well with an exceptional aberration of Mrs. Indira Gandhi who promoted national emergency (1975-1977). This was despite Churchill's observation that democratic reins were impossible beyond the Suez. He added, "India must be governed by old principles."[7] How well Indian system has worked and works now, or what are its deficiencies, can only be known when we compare ourselves with the developed democracies like the US or the UK or the rest in Europe.

However, if we compare ourselves with the democracies of developing world, we are in for a pleasant surprise. If we go to countries in South Asia or Southeast Asia for instance, barring Singapore, informed public would urge their own government to emulate the example set by India. Bangladesh Parliamentarians often refer to Indian reforms to plead for similar changes in their country.[8] Dennis Kux, an India watcher in the US, after elaborately discussing the birth pangs suffered by India in the immediate aftermath of partition in 1947, and with "the staggering problems of trying to overcome mass poverty and illiteracy, representative government has taken firm roots during the past half century. Among the new nations of Asia and Africa, India stands out as a success story for democracy."[9]

Indian Parliamentary System

In the Constitution of India, Parliamentary form of government has been provided at the federal level and has also been repeated at the states' level. India has followed the British Parliamentary system. Despite all the praise, as a political system, Parliamentary democracy that works in India suffers from two flaws—Frequent Elections and the Model Code of Conduct. These became visible since the 4th General Elections held in 1967. Until then the nation had experienced under the Congress Party, what is called "One Party Dominance".

These flaws affect the efficacy of not only democracy but also its reliability in providing good governance as well. It is these flaws that often make educated Indian leaders to be critical of the working of democracy in India. Former PM, A.B. Vajpayee, for instance, had said a few months before the fall of his government in April 1999: Democracy in India "appears to have become a hollow shell" with "elections reduced to a farce". In the General Elections of 1999 he was returned by the people but he continued to maintain that "outer shell of democracy is, no doubt, intact but it appears to be moth-eaten from inside."[10] Then, what are these two flaws?

Frequent Elections

First, frequent elections necessitated by the system have affected the working of democracy and its claim to deliver good governance. Under the Constitution, elections have to be held, both at the federal and state levels, once in every five years. But, the Constitution does not guarantee a fixed term of five years to the House called Lok Sabha at the federal level and Legislative Assemblies in the states. In the Parliamentary system, as it grew in the United Kingdom, has an executive which is a small committee of the Parliament itself. If one looks at the evolution of the Parliamentary System, it becomes clear that since the Executive advises the King in the discharge of his powers, people's representatives who sit in the House of Commons retain the right to pass a no confidence motion against the King's advisers, and replace the executive committee.

Over the centuries, the King has lost most of his powers, and the cabinet is the beneficiary. With the development of the party system, political parties have exercised the right to pass a no-confidence motion against the government of the day. Hence, today the parliamentary system is conducive to an inducement of an election any time if the governments at the federal level and states do not have a working majority.

In borrowing the parliamentary system from Britain, the Constituent Assembly did without much understanding the systemic suitability, to a nation like India with multi-ethnic, multi-religious, multi-linguistic, multi-caste and multi-regional differences. In such situations, since Indian politicians have not gone through the historic experiences of development of the Parliamentary System, the concept of 'opposition' and 'no confidence motion' are deeply rooted in their psyche. They get easily tempted to pass a 'no confidence' motion against the government if it does not enjoy an absolute majority. The members sitting in the opposition have then one point programme: Get rid of the government from power! Thus all instrumentalities of destabilisation of an elected government, like political defections, inducement of party splits, mergers, bribery, offer of positions become normal.

In such situations, what comes next does not matter to them. Thus, for instance, during the tenure of NDA-I, late Madhavrao Scindia, the then deputy leader of the Congress Party in the Lok Sabha, spoke (in May 2001) of the inevitable fall of the NDA government. He said that "NDA government cannot survive too long." When asked by a correspondent as to what happens if it fails, he said, in a demonstration of the most irresponsible attitude, that there were possibilities of "an alternative combination...or *finally, it could be back to polls.*"[11] (Emphasis supplied)

In Indian federal system, states also have a similar system. In the absence of a clear majority, the 'opposition' in the States too plays similar games of overthrowing an elected government. This creates a need for holding fresh elections. Obviously, then state elections do not synchronise among the states and elections at the level of states do not synchronise with the election at the federal level. To this list of elections, if we add elections to the various municipal councils, corporations, Zillah Parishads and Panchayats, elections would become national festivals that can be witnessed by voters in villages, towns and cities on an almost everyday basis!

The Executive branch in the parliamentary system is controlled by elected politicians; making the politicians in power constantly involved in electioneering leaving them very little time to attend to administration in the executive branch. Under these circumstances they are least concerned about good governance—let alone governance itself. Thus the fact is that the political system adopted by the nation directly damages the cause of democracy as well as good governance.

Model Code of Conduct

Second flaw obstructing good governance by the Indian democracy is the Model Code of Conduct (MCC)[12] drawn up and enforced by the Election Commission of India (ECI). MCC is based on the study of past behaviour of politicians in power. During the 1971 elections at the federal level, for instance, soon after her decisive victory in the Bangladesh War, Indira Gandhi, on behalf of the Congress Party went on laying foundation stones for various projects throughout the country. Such actions on the part of the ruling party, obviously gives it an advantage, though on a short term basis.

One needs to avoid such situations to make elections appear to be fair to all contestants and all parties without giving them any cause to complain. MCC in essence, aims to provide a level playing field to all political parties contesting elections at the state as well as the Federal levels. If a chief minister, for instance, uses state helicopter to campaign, and a member of an opposition party has to campaign on his bicycle, there is an inherent disadvantage suffered by the latter affecting his political fortune in the elections.

Whatever may have been its legitimate concerns to begin with, today the MCC acts as a disincentive to perform and provide services to community in Indian democracy. In implementing certain guidelines of the MCC in the recent times, the ECI has carried the provisions of the MCC to ridiculously dangerous levels from the point of view of good governance. This includes bringing to grinding halt ongoing projects which were approved much earlier. That leaves roads dug up and left unattended because of MCC as elections are announced. Similarly, if a decision has been taken by the government in the normal course, its implementation should not be held up just because an election is going to be held. This practice harms public-utility projects like opening a bridge constructed or sanction and release of land for a school playground. Such actions, intended or unintended, lead to delays denying benefits of good governance!

Damages Caused

These two systemic fault-lines in Indian parliamentary system, viz. frequent elections and model code of conduct, in our opinion, cause, either jointly or severally, certain damages to good governance in a welfare democracy. The very nature of Parliamentary system causes frequent elections and in a federal system such elections are held many more times, as many as states go for elections. This causes damages to democratic good governance in a variety of ways. These factors are further compounded by the faulty and unimaginative implementation of MCC, as it results in delays in providing services to the civil society, thus affecting good governance. Without claiming to be exhaustive, some of the well-established types of damages caused to the effective working of good governance and democracy are briefly discussed below.

Politicking, More Than Politics

The Indian Parliamentary democracy suffers from too many occasions of electioneering and provides opportunities for indulging in politicking by politicians. It is true that politics is a democratic need and a necessity without which democracy cannot function. Here 'politics' is defined as 'authoritative allocation of values' in a society. Good Governance depends on good politics.

On the other hand, 'politicking' can be defined as pursuit of political activities and goals to promote oneself or one's own policies more with an eye on one's family, relatives and friends' good, if not only for individual good. Hence, that leaves very little time for focusing on good governance and providing good administration services to the citizens even if a politician is genuinely committed for the good of the society. Thus, through the systemic features, Parliamentary system motivates politicians to indulge more in politicking from the day—one in office rather than in politics. During the periods between PMs at the federal level or CMs at the states' level, election as the leader by the parliamentary party and their going back to people to seek a fresh mandate, allows them spend more time in retaining their chair and campaigning in elections than serving the nation.

Administration Delays in Delivery of Services

Greater the commitment of the political leadership to the welfare of the society, the greater is the need for a large bureaucracy to translate its commitment to provide good governance. Bureaucrats who man the administrative machinery in various departments of the government—from IAS officers at the top to ordinary assistants at the bottom, have generally no incentives to carry on the service to the community when the political system is going through the electoral process. At the least, at the higher level of bureaucratic pyramid, officers are uncertain as to who will be returned by the voters as their new masters! Often political differences between the parties—ruling and in opposition—could bring a punishment or reward for the work done by them during the tenure of government led by different political parties.

Wastage of Scarce Resources

Frequent elections make the government to provide more funds to the Election Commission. That simply means that whatever could have been spent for the welfare of the people, perforce will be diverted to conduct elections. An election to the Lok Sabha at the turn of the twenty first century cost about Rs. 800 crore. The election held in 2009 cost the people of the country Rs. 1400 crore. The election of 2014 is estimated to have emptied around Rs. 2500 crore from the consolidated fund of India.

On the other hand, application of the model code of conduct during the electoral politics, in effect does not lead to spending of resources raised for projects from the people as taxes or from the global lending agencies like World Bank and the International Monetary Fund, or several others with interest, leading to additional tax burden on voters!

Thus, according to a report, just two weeks before the end of the Financial Year 2016-17 in the state of Maharashtra, out of a sum of Rs. 89,778 crores allocated for development, only Rs. 46,809 crore were spent.[13] The report says that the officials blamed the imposition of Model Code of Conduct for nearly 90 days during the BMC elections.[14]

Politics Governed by Money Power

Electoral politics are mainly driven by money power. Money is mother's milk of politics today in all democracies; India is no exception. Frequent elections need political parties to raise and spend funds frequently. In the absence of state funding of elections, money is raised through donations by all political parties from the persons chosen for implementing government projects. States like Bihar had in the past ministers who publicly said that getting a cut of ten per cent in amount paid to a company or a contractor for executing a project is their legitimate due. Privately, many MLAs and BMC Corporators have admitted the prevalence of such practice in Mumbai city as well.

At the level of ordinary citizens, the delay in getting essential services because of frequent elections and enforcement of MCC, inevitably forces the citizens into bribery and corruption to get their basic needs. Many citizens have also been forced by circumstances to bribe the municipal officials to get death certificates of their deceased parents. The rates of bribe go up if the officials come to know that the applicant is an NRI! to cite another example, the Central Board of Secondary Education (CBSE) insists on a certificate from the local authorities stating that the water provided to the children in the school is potable water! Trustees of an educational institution are told that the Rules do not authorise them to issue such a certificate. The required certificate is obtained by an agent for a monetary consideration! It is the author's personal experience that transfer a piece of land reserved for school run by an Educational Trust by the government way back 1995 has not in reality taken place because the trust has refused to indulge in bribery.[15]

Credibility of Democracy Questioned

Frequent elections discredit democracy. Way back in the 1950s, Ivor Jennings wrote: "Frequent resignations involve frequent party splits and party splits lead to short and weak governments, which in turn lead to distrust of the democratic system."[16] If he were to write it today, he would have also added that it denies the government an opportunity to pursue good governance. In a recent incident, a woman voter in Assam expressed her lethargy in voting and when she was asked by a correspondent: did you vote in the recent bye-elections? Her natural answer was "no". Too often voting is also a tiresome activity! This shows natural apathy of voters to frequent elections. This will naturally show a decline of voters' participation in the electoral process.

Remedial Actions Proposed

These fault-lines can be corrected and damages can be checked to a great extent, if not eliminated altogether, by adopting certain reforms *within* the existing Parliamentary System. These reforms can be implemented either through a law of the Parliament or through constitutional amendments as may be considered necessary by legal experts.

One Nation, One People, One Election

In recent times, the need for reforming parliamentary system's feature of making the nation to go through the ordeal of frequent elections was highlighted by Prime Minister Narendra Modi more than once. He called for a national debate on the subject. This was also approvingly referred by President Pranab Mukherjee.[17] Both of them supported the catchy slogan: "One Nation One Election".[18] As a matter of fact, this idea was also placed before the nation by the former Prime Minister Atal Behari Vajpayee. While speaking at the golden jubilee celebrations of the ECI, he had proposed "a fixed tenure for our Parliament and State Legislatures is essential for our democratic system to mature and *deliver good governance.*"[19] (Emphasis supplied).

Expressed Difficulties

Many have expressed their opposition to the above proposal. In every nation there is always a vast majority of people, who are afraid to experiment with the unknown. They say: known devil is better than the unknown one. While a nation cannot progress if it is not prepared to experiment with the unknown, the stakeholders do not wish to lose the advantages of the known system. In the Constituent Assembly of India, eminent thinkers like, Prof. K.T. Shah and H.V. Kamath had suggested that India may go in for a Presidential form of government, which incidentally, is also democratic like the parliamentary form!

But men with *status quo* mind-set preferred to stick to the Parliamentary form. Thus, on their behalf K.M. Munshi, for instance, said: After thirty to forty years of experience with such a system, "why should we go back upon the tradition that has been built for over hundred years and try a novel experiment...?" On behalf of the majority, Munshi had claimed that the Parliamentary system has been providing "strongest" and "classic executive."[20] However, this author's contrary views are reinforced by what S.C. Kashyap, who wrote: "The framers of the Constitution neither had time nor the interest to conceive of a structure that kept in mind the future of India and which was in sync with the culture and views of our people."[21]

Regional Parties Likely to Oppose

Views have been expressed by politicians that regional parties which are now in power like Trinamul Congress in West Bengal, or AIADMK in Tamil Nadu or Biju Janata Dal (BJD) in Odisha feel that if all elections are held at one time throughout the nation, citizens as voters throughout the country might be carried away by the campaign issues raised by the national parties.

In this author's opinion, the proposed fixed tenure to the elected body results in denial of political accountability of the Council of Ministers to the elected House at the federal or the state level in a parliamentary system. The core belief ingrained in the minds of those who practice parliamentary form of government is the question of executive accountability to the elected representatives of the people and to make it responsive to people's loss of confidence in the Council of Ministers is to remove them from office by expressing their lack of confidence in them by a 'no confidence' motion. If a fixed term is provided to the elected house, neither the house can remove the cabinet nor can the cabinet threaten to cut short tenure of the elected house by its dissolution if the members become recalcitrant to leadership of the executive where it is sure of public support to their proposed policy.

Switch Over to Presidential System

A fixed tenure to the executive and legislature is the basic feature of Presidential system. Thus, from time to time different politicians, administrators and academics have pointed out one aspect of the question under discussion here for remedial action. One early reform this author had suggested initially was to try to reform parliamentary system rather than reject it, when Barrister Antulay had publicly proposed introduction of Presidential system, after Indira Gandhi was re-elected early in 1980 with a decisive mandate after having rejected her in 1977.[22] This author could not accept the reasons advanced by Antulay as real; because the general public had a suspicion then that it was an effort to perpetuate Mrs. Gandhi's rule.[23]

Some may feel rightly even today that a switch over to presidential system might be a better option to meet the challenges posed by frequent elections in our Parliamentary system. There are many in this country, who fear that the proposed 'One Nation one Election' itself is a precursor to switch over to Presidential System. For instance, the NDA-I government led by Vajpayee proposed the appointment of a commission to review the constitution and proposed the name of former judge of Supreme Court, Venkatachaliaya. However, the latter put a condition that he would accept the appointment, only if the PM gave an assurance to him that purpose of constitutional review was not to propose a Presidential system!

Hence, to ensure that history does not repeat itself on this subject, Prime Minister Modi could adopt a via media to achieve nation's goal of safeguarding the purpose of government in Indian democracy to provide for good governance.

Via Media

Three alternatives could be considered as the first stage of reforms towards the ultimate goal of switch over to a Presidential system. First: electing members of the Rajya Sabha at the federal level and the Legislative Councils in states directly by the people. Second: direct election of Governors to the states, and the third: based on the efficacy of these measures and based on whether the nation is happy with the decisions taken to achieve a minimum degree of minimising of elections in the country or whether it would like to switch over to a presidential system. the three options are briefly elaborated here.

Direct Election to the Upper Houses

One may find that the proposal of direct elections to the Rajya Sabha and Legislative Councils in the states, wherever they exist, might have no direct bearing on good governance. But a deeper analysis might show that such a system will have a direct bearing on the strengthening of democracy in India; and whatever strengthens democracy strengthens good governance. At present these members are indirectly elected. As a rule, whichever body is indirectly elected is prone to greater corruption than the directly elected bodies. In the direct elections those who aspire to get elected have to seek popular votes. Those who get elected through direct elections have a greater sense of commitment to the people. In the indirect elections, the elected representatives are insensitive to peoples' grievances as they owe their seat in the indirectly elected body to the party high command. And in many cases they are elected because of their money power.

These facts are borne out by the experiences of the US Senate until the 19th century and the Rajya Sabha in India as of now. The US Senate was indirectly elected by the state legislatures until the passage of 17th Constitutional Amendment in 1912-13. As long as they were indirectly elected, with the industrialisation and growth of the party system, they began to represent party bosses or various lobbies like steel trust, sugar trust, railroad trust etc. The Senate came to be called the millionaires club.[24] After the Senators came to be elected directly, they have become very powerful; often better representatives of the state's interests and often providing presidential timber.

Rajya Sabha is in no way different. Even now it continues to be an indirectly elected body. Seats are literally purchased by industrialists like Vijay Mallya or R.P. Goenka and several others.[25] Though the electors are state MLAs, seats are allocated by the party bosses. If Rajya Sabha is also directly elected with only two members representing a state irrespective of the size of the state as in the case of the US Senate, Indian federal structure could also become a vibrant concept.

Elected Governors

In our present parliamentary system, Chief Executives at the federal and state levels come from the elected houses, Lok Sabha and the Legislative Assemblies of the respective states. But, there is also a governor nominated by the federal government in every state as its representative. This is a British vestige, as when imperial government gave certain powers to the states they also desired to protect the interest of the Colonial power. But, do we need it now; seventy years after independence?

By a constitutional amendment we can introduce a directly elected governor as the Chief Executive in a State.[26] He will enjoy a fixed term of five years, during which he can serve the population of state without fearing any destabilisation by an opponent. Opposition candidates have to wait till next election to get into power. This experience, say for ten years, should convince political parties and a majority of the people who think that in India "a known devil is better" on the suitability of a change in the system of single executive rather than a plural executive as at present.

Presidential Democracy

Ultimately, a Presidential form of government could very well take care of minimising the number of elections. In the American Presidential System it is said: From the President to the dog catcher in the county, are all elected on the same day, with the exception of bye elections in the event of demise of a sitting senator. Such a system gives a nationally elected President to serve the people during the period without worrying about constantly of next election. This form is better suited to promote democracy and through it good governance in a nation like India.[27]

Notes

1. A visit to a nationalised bank or a ration office in India will show that the service providers are engrossed in talking over the cell phone rather than looking at the visitor. While this author has personally experienced such a situation, there are many such reports; *see* a recent report of women members of a rationing office in Mulund (West) selling saris during office hours. *Home Times,* 6-12 May, 2017.
2. Maharashtra Government has enacted the Right to Services Act and has recently appointed its retiring Chief Secretary to the government as the first Commissioner. Thus, the Chief Secretary who could not ensure that services were properly provided by the government while he was in government service, gets the benefit of continuing in service as the Chief Commissioner of Services, with a mandate that services are promptly provided! Isn't it an irony of good governance?
3. In 1983, this author delivered a lecture to the bureaucrats in Mantralaya under the auspices of the Maharashtra Regional Branch of the Indian Institute of Public Administration. After listening to the talk, many IAS officers agreed with this author's criticism of the Indian bureaucracy. (*See* for the text of lecture, "Personnel Behaviour in the American and Indian Public Administration: Some comparative views," in R.C. Iyer and S.S. Gadkari (Eds.) *Personnel Management in Public Administration* (Mumbai: The Indian Institute of Public Administration, Maharashtra Branch, 1983) pp. 63-69.
4. Quoted in P.M. Kamath, "The New World Order: Who Orders, and for Whose Good?" in Kausar J. Azam (Ed.), *Rediscovering America: American Studies in the New Century,* New Delhi (2001), South Asian Publishers. p. 235. *See* also for greater details, Francis Fukuyama, "*Second Thoughts: the End of History 10 years Later*," NPQ, Summer, 1999.
5. From the *Web of Government* (1947) quoted in P.M. Kamath, "The Emerging

Challenges to Indian Democracy: Is National Politics Turning Anarchic?" in Debabrata Panda and N.P. Chaubey (Eds.) *Democracy, Peoples' Development and Culture* (Allahabad: Indian Academy of Social Sciences, 2006), p. 63.

6. In this author's view, post-National Emergency, this awareness has increased. Any repetition of another emergency is unlikely to happen.
7. Note. 5, p. 62.
8. *See* P. M. Kamath, "Secular democracy in India: the Domestic and Regional Challenges," in the Institute of Regional Studies (Ed.), *Current Domestic Policy Challenges and Prospects in South Asia,* Islamabad, 2003, Institute of Regional Studies, p. 30.
9. "India Today: A rising democracy," in *Great Decisions,* New York (2002): Foreign Policy Association, p. 58.
10. Quoted in, P. M. Kamath, "System Turning Anarchic?" *Observer of Business and Politics,* 15 August, 2000.
11. *The Hindu* (online edition), 4 May, 2001.
12. *See* for details, Election Commission of India, Model Code of Conduct for the Guidance of Political Parties and Candidates, 2007 (Available at http://eci.nic.in/eci_main/faq_mcc.pdf)
13. *See* Sandeep Ashar's report, "In Maharashtra, over 50 per cent development fund yet to be used," in *Indian Express* (Mumbai), 14 March, 2017.
14. *Ibid.*
15. *See* Press Report in *Lok Satta* (Mumbai), 26 February, 2011.
16. *Cabinet Government,* Cambridge (1951), Cambridge University Press, p. 261.
17. "Centre seeks views on simultaneous polls to Lok Sabha, Assembliles" (Available at http://www.thehindu.com/news/nationalCentre-seeks-views-on-simultaneous-polls-to-Lok-Sabha-Assemblies/article14630817.ece)
18. "Centre seeks views on simultaneous polls to Lok Sabha, Assemblies", 9 September, 2016. (Available at http://www.thehindu.com/news/national/Centre-seeks-views-on-simultaneous-polls-to-Lok-Sabha-Assemblies/article14630817.ece)
19. *The Times of India* (Mumbai), 3 August, 1999.
20. *Constitutional Assembly Debates,* Vol. VII, p. 984. *See* also M.V. Pylee, *Constitutional Government in India,* Bombay (1977), Asia Publishing House, p. 324.
21. "An unfulfilled dream," *Sunday Times of India* (Mumbai), 16 August, 2003.
22. *See* P. M. Kamath, *Indian Politics under Mrs. Gandhi: Reflective Essays,* New Delhi (1993): South Asian Publishers, pp. 106-119.
23. During the period of emergency, in an interview with Kuldip Nayar, Sanjay Gandhi had said that his plan was to indefinitely extend emergency, get rid of democratic institutions and establish Indira's dictatorship forever. (Avalaible at http://guruprasad.net/posts/1975-77-emergency-excesses-sanjay-gandhis-role/)
24. *See* P.M. Kamath, "Games People Play," *Mid-Day,* 4 April, 2000.

25. *See* P.M. Kamath, "Council of States: Let People elect," *Observer of Economics and Politics*, 14 April, 2000.
26. When this author had advocated reforming parliamentary system before moving to Presidential System, he had suggested an indirectly elected Governor with the participation of elected members of the State Legislature and Local bodies. *See* P.M. Kamath, "How Best to Choose Governors?", *Times of India*, 27 July, 1984.
27. This author had carried out a UGC-funded project on "Presidential System for the Promotion of Two-Party System and National Unity in India."

5

Good Governance

From Kautilya's *Arthashastra* to Narendra Modi

Vasundhara Mohan

"Good Governance is perhaps the single most important factor in eradicating poverty and promoting development."
(*Kofi Annan,* UN Secretary General)

Introduction

The era of Kings and Monarchs has long gone, except in some countries where they continue to head governments. Present day democracies are headed by elected Presidents and Prime Ministers. However, the principles of governance expounded by Kautilya (also known as Chanakya) around 350 BC and the aims and objectives of governance continue to hold good even today. Kautilya's *Arthashastra* (meaning Scripture of Wealth) deals extensively with aspects of political, economic and social management.

Kautilya's Concept of Good Governance

Kautilya's *Arthashastra* had maintained that the state or government has a vital role to play in maintaining the well-being and material status of both the nation and its people. Holding that good governance is paramount, Kautilya had suggested built-in checks and balances in the systems and procedures for the containment of malpractices.

Elaborating on the factors that go into Good governance, *Arthashastra* held that first of these factors is the leader, who is held responsible for everything that happens in the society. Kautilya held that the leader must exhibit a number of virtues. The leader's main goal being the maintenance of the welfare of the people (*Yogakshema*), the leader must work for this goal disregarding his own needs. The leader should not only render service to the people but should defer to the law and be virtuous. Other traits in a leader are that he should be active and hardworking to set an example to his subordinates. Most important of all, if the leader were to fight corruption in the society, he should be morally upright, honest and trustworthy.

Arthashastra stipulates that besides the leader heading the government, the officials who implement the policies of the government should also possess the same qualities and strive for the betterment of the lives of the people. Interestingly, in stating the dimensions of a good governance, the World Bank called for "a bureaucracy imbued with a professional ethos; an executive arm of government accountable for its actions; and a strong civil society participating in public affairs; and all behaving under the rule of law." It is only when the officials are imbued with professional ethos that they will feel responsible not only for formulating the budget of a project but also for overseeing the implementation of a given project at every stage for its effective implementation for the public-good.

Arthashastra requires that a successful government shall implement projects for improving the nation. The most important of these is the prioritisation of education in as much as a well-educated and trained human capital is essential for the economy of a country. In the contemporary period, the UNDP states that Good governance lies in "assuring that everyone, irrespective of social or economic status, has a voice in governing and receives just, fair, equitable treatment. Good governance is, among other things, participatory, transparent and accountable. It is also effective and equitable and promotes the rule of law. Good governance ensures that political, social and economic priorities are based on broad consensus in society and that the voices of the poorest and the most vulnerable are heard in decision-making over the allocation of development resources."

A government has also to keep a close watch on the performance of its officials by gathering feedback from the nation's stakeholders periodically. An evaluation achieved through the feedback serves as a critique for the administration, forming the basis for improvement. Lastly, although the *Arthashastra*'s main goal and responsibility was the welfare of the people, Kautilya includes rules in his treatise for the maintenance of the environment and other living things.

The cardinal principle of economic administration was laid down in Kautilya's *Arthashastra* in the following words:

> "The root of wealth is economic activity and lack of it brings material distress. In the absence of fruitful economic activity, both current prosperity and future growth are in danger of destruction. The King shall populate the countryside by creating new villages on virgin lands or reviving abandoned village sites."

According to the *Arthashastra*, there is a strong connection between good governance and the economy of a nation when it states that "the end is economic governance while political governance is the means." It means that proper management and good governance have a direct effect on the economic aspects of a nation. But, as economic objectives are not realised in the absence of political ones, political governance becomes an end and economic governance the means. "*The end justifies the means*", this is supposed to be the basis of Kautilya's philosophy. Political power and material wealth according to Kautilya are the means and ends of governance.

Finally, Good governance is associated with democracy and good civil rights, with transparency, rule of law, and efficient public services, and active participation of the people (through their representatives) in the framing of Laws and overseeing the performance of the government. The elected representatives are expected to act as a watch dog of the performance of the government.

The concept of Good governance as elaborated in Kautilya's *Arthashastra* is aimed at ensuring the welfare of the people. "In the happiness of the King's subjects lies his happiness; in their welfare, his welfare. Whatever pleases him personally, he shall not consider as good, but whatever makes his subjects happy, he shall consider good." Similar sentiments were expressed when Mahatma Gandhi stated: Before you do anything, stop and recall the face of the poorest most helpless destitute person you have seen and ask yourself, "Is what I am about to do going to help him?"

Modern Concepts and Definitions of Good Governance

In modern times, the concept of good governance emerged at the end of the 1980s; at a time of unprecedented political changes like the collapse of the Berlin Wall and the disintegration of the Soviet Union. These events led to the decay of the political and economic alliances of the Eastern block leading to a serious discussion on how a state has to be designed in order to achieve (economic) development, i.e. a discussion on good governance. In a 1989 study the term "governance" was first used to describe the need for institutional reform and a better and more efficient public sector in Sub-Saharan countries.

World Bank conceptually defines "governance (as opposed to "good" governance) as the rule of the rulers, typically within a given set of rules. One might conclude that governance is the *process*—by which authority is conferred on rulers, by which they make the rules, and by which those rules are enforced and modified. Thus, understanding governance requires an identification of rulers and the ruled, as well as the various processes by which they are selected, defined, and linked together and with the society generally." Thus, Governance refers to the manner in which power is exercised in utilizing the country's economic and social resources for its development and for the common good. Good governance is associated with democracy and good civil rights, with transparency, with the rule of law, and with efficient public services. For a government to be "good", it is essential that all the systems and subsystems of the government are efficient, effective, economic, and meet the expectations of the citizens. In 1994, the World Bank defined governance as one epitomized by predictable, open, and enlightened policymaking (that is, transparent processes); a bureaucracy imbued with a professional ethos; an executive arm of government accountable for its actions; and a strong civil society participating in public affairs; and all behaving under the rule of law. World Bank's definition is no different from what Kautilya said centuries ago.

However, Good governance cannot be left entirely to the rulers. Citizens' involvement is critical for ensuring good governance in terms of enhancing democratic governance, improved service delivery, and fostering empowerment. Otherwise known as Social accountability, it refers to the extent and capacity of the citizens to hold the state and service providers accountable and make them responsive to needs of citizens and beneficiaries. Social accountability encompasses initiatives that focus on citizens as the ultimate stakeholders and is based on the principles of transparency, accountability, and participation. Social accountability approaches and tools also strengthen the capacity of non-governmental organisations, the media, local communities, and the private sector to hold authorities accountable for better development results.

As far as the modern definition of good governance goes, there is no single accepted one. World Bank and other multilateral development banks are concerned with economic institutions and public sector management, including transparency and accountability, regulatory reform, and public sector skills and leadership. But for others like the United Nations, European Commission and OECD, the indicators of good governance are democratic governance and human rights, about which the International Financial Institutions are not much bothered. Unlike good concepts, good governance has different definitions. A country might be having good governance in respect to some characteristics but doing poorly with respect to others. John Healey and Mark Robinson define "Good government" as follows:

> "It implies a high level of organisational effectiveness in relation to policy-formulation and the policies actually pursued, especially in the conduct of economic policy and its contribution to growth, stability and popular welfare. Good government also implies accountability, transparency, participation, openness and the rule of law. It does not necessarily presuppose a value judgement, for example, a healthy respect for civil and political liberties, although good government tends to be a prerequisite for political legitimacy."

Thus, good governance does not stop at efficient economic management; it is something more than that. "It is a more broad reform strategy to make government more open, responsive, accountable, democratic, as well as strengthen institutions of civil society and regulate private sector. Good governance is a combination of efficiency concerns of public management and accountability concerns of governance."

Good Governance and Nehru

Independent India that Nehru inherited was beset with enormous problems in terms of the size of its population, poverty and non-existent industrialisation, poor infrastructure etc., Also, the British leaving him no tradition of good governance to fall back on, Nehru had to reinvent the art of Indian statesmanship in a new world order.

A staunch believer in democracy and secularism, for Nehru democracy was not just about the right to vote, but also having the economic means to leverage one's democratic rights. Nehru was also a strong advocate of the *Panchayati Raj*, and believed that development should not be dictated from above, but come up from below. Though he initiated the Panchayati Raj system in 1957, with his death in 1964, *Panchayati Raj* also met a slow death and was revived by Rajiv Gandhi in 1993. A firm believer in secularism, Nehru fought for a secular India. He also believed in socialism based on democracy and non-violence, leading to the establishment of a cooperative, socialist commonwealth. He advocated for the abolition of the *Zamindari* system of landownership, and the rapid acceleration of industrialisation through central planning. His socialistic bent of mind did not permit the growth of private sector.

Unfortunately, the administrative set up established by the British was largely left untouched during Nehru's period and administrative reforms were slow to take off, if there had been any. Nehru's successors proved to be poor caretakers of his legacy. the cooperatives and local institutions set up during Nehru's time slowly became more and more bureaucratised and fell victim to graft and rent-seeking. Along with *Panchayati Raj*, the bottom-up development slowly withered away and a new form of corporate feudalism emerged in its place. the quality of public schooling sharply declined along with many other pro-poor programmes he had set up.

Governance Under A.B. Vajpayee

The NDA government under Atal Behari Vajpayee accepted the need for economic reforms initiated by the previous government and pushed it into the second generation with enhanced vigour. Under his guidance, the Department of Administrative Reforms and Public Grievance prepared a 9-point action plan. This included an affective and speedy redressal of public grievances, empowerment of elected rural and urban bodies, review of laws, rules and regulations, transparency and right to information, action for tackling corruption etc. But, nothing concrete emerged, which was attributed to the inertia at all levels. Such inertia has ensured that the recommendations of various committees, commissions etc., remained in files. Under the circumstances, people came to the conclusion that any good that would happen in the society will be totally on account of the independent judiciary. On the other hand, civil society organisations and social movements were able to make a major dent.

Good Governance and Narendra Modi

Since his election campaign days in 2014, Narendra Modi has been talking about Good Governance. Following the victory of the Bharatiya Janata Party at the 2014 polls and his election as the Prime Minister, Narendra Modi declared:

> "Good Governance is the key to a nation's progress. Our government is committed to providing a transparent and accountable administration which works for the betterment and welfare of the common citizen. "Citizen-First" is our *mantra*, our motto and our guiding principle. It has been my dream to bring government closer to our citizens, so, that they become active participants in the governance process."

Narendra Modi felt that an important step for Good Governance is simplification of procedures and processes in the Government so as to make the entire system transparent and faster. He stressed on the development of a relationship between the citizens and the government based on trust. He started doing away with cumbersome and outdated legislations which no longer had any relevance. Realising the importance of redressal of public grievances for a responsive administration, he instructed all the Ministries to ensure that redressal of public grievances received the highest priority.

A strong believer in technology, Narendra Modi said that technology is an empowering tool for the citizens and an accountability medium for the government. He expressed his desire to bridge the divide between the government and the citizens with the help of technology. His aim is to transform the country into a digitally empowered society as it would ensure that Government services are available to citizens electronically. In his Independence Day speech on 15 August, 2016, Narendra Modi re-emphasized his slogan of good governance, saying accountability and responsibility are key to attain this. Modi said *Swaraj* is about empowering citizens and improving their quality of life and that his government was committed to bring that change to every citizen of the country.

Conclusion

It has been ages since Kautilya's *Arthashastra* elucidated the importance for and conditions of a good governance. Have we achieved even a small percentage of Kautilya's prescription; or those of the World Bank and others for that matter? It has also been almost three years since Narendra Modi started emphasising on and promising good governance. Has anything changed?

- Corruption still remains a malaise in the Indian society. If a given leader is a part of corruption in the country, there is no way he can achieve the goal of serving the people. We do not propose to cite examples; there are too many. It is for this reason that the *Arthashastra* invoked the people to elect a leader worthy enough to be entrusted the welfare of the nation. In a society ridden with religion and caste considerations, it is well neigh impossible to elect of leader with the highest integrity.
- The elected representatives continue to fail their electorate. They even fail to attend the parliament or assembly sessions regularly and take part in the discussions. How can they perform their constitutional duties? (According to one source, the median attendance of Members of Lok Sabha is about 82.5%, increasing to about 84.3% during budget sessions).
- Many legislators do not take their responsibilities to their constituencies seriously and hardly bother themselves with the development of their own constituencies and let a large percentage of their constituency development funds remain unutilized, while those who elected them have been crying hoarse for drinking water, schools, roads and electricity.
- The unruly behaviour of some of the members of the Parliament/Assembly, both inside and outside the parliament/ Assembly, their irresponsible comments even on sensitive issue leave much to be desired.
- Stressing the significance of training and learning, Kautilya stated that investment in human capital, especially in higher education, would have a greater impact on the growth and development of the economy. But, in India reports have repeatedly highlighted the pathetic conditions of schools, and paucity of teachers especially in rural areas. It is not that the

elected representatives and officers are not aware of the problems. Such shortcomings are taken for granted.

- Because of apathy, lethargy and corruption, a number of government projects, however, well-intentioned, continue to over run their budgets or the assets created under the projects remain sub-standard.
- *Arthashastra* has emphasized on agriculture and stresses on the importance of irrigation and providing amenities for agriculture on a priority basis. If only the governments take remedial measures to help the agriculturists in time, why would hundreds of them slip into poverty, helplessness, indebtedness etc., and commit suicide?

We now have a Prime Minister who talks about good governance almost in everyone of his public speeches. He has raised the global acceptability rate of India. He wants to make India digital and promote India as a global manufacturing hub. His policies may push India's technological prowess but will these measures ensure good governance? It may be recalled that after the Gujarat riots in 2002, the then Prime Minister Atal Behari Vajpayee had advised Narendra Modi, then Chief Minister of Gujarat, to scrupulously follow *Raj Dharma* "without showing any discrimination between the people on the basis of caste, creed or religion." In other words, "*Sarve Jana Sukhina Bhavantu*" (let all the people be happy) is the essence of Good governance. We feel that the lackadaisical attitude of the politicians, bureaucrats and others is equally responsible for the absence of Good governance. Proper attitude/mind-set is *sine qua non* with Good governance. Simultaneously, the society itself has to share the blame for its lack of enthusiasm, social responsibility, social behaviour, ambition and "could not careless" attitude. What would one call if a group of people watch and even video graph if a girl is being molested in broad day light? Why cannot the Bangalore citizens haul up the City Corporation if the lakes are burning? Good Governance is like a clap: it takes two hands to clap; both the government and concerned citizens. An all-round change is needed before we can expect Good governance.

References

Ali, S.S. (2006) Kautilya and the concept of good governance, in *Indian Journal of Political Science*, Vol. XVII, No. 2, April-June.

Gisselquist, Rachel (2012), *What is Good Governance*, United Nations University, 9 February.(Available at https://unu.edu/publications/articles/what-does-good-governance-mean.html)

Maldonado, Nicole. The World Bank's Evolving Concept of Good Governance and its Impact on Human Rights, *Paper presented at the Doctoral workshop on Development and International Organizations*, Stockholm, Sweden, May 29-30, 2010.

Mishra, Anju. *Kautilya's Arthashastra*, (Available at http://anujamisra.blogspot.in/2010/01/kautilyas-arthashastra.html).

PM's Message to the Nation on Good Governance Day, 25 December, 2014. (Available at http://www.narendramodi.in/pms-message-to-the-nation-on-good-governance-7080).

Roffeisen, Crees (2016) *How Nehru Shaped India's Development*, September 18. (Available at https://www.linkedin.com/pulse/how-nehru-shaped-indias-development-cees-roffelsen-m-a-%E7%BD%97%E5%87%AF%E6%96%AF-).

See, http://theballot.in/lok-sabha-attendance/

See, https://www.slideshare.net/CreateDemandNow/good-governance-3

Sharma, Dr. Sanjeev Kumar. (2005), Indian Idea of Good Governance: Revisiting Kautilya's *Arthashastra*. *Dynamics of Administration*, Lucknow, Vol. XVII, Nos. 1-2, January-December pp. 8-19.

Singh, Ravindra Nath (2009) Good Governance: A *sine qua non* for Economic Development, in *Governance, Democracy and Development* (Eds.) Anil Kumar Thakur and Krishnanand Yadav, Delhi : Deep & Deep Publications Pvt. Ltd., pp. 102, 105-106.

Understanding the Concept of Governance, in *Governance Barometer: Policy Guidelines for Good Governance* (Available at https://www.gdrc.org/u-gov/governance-understand.html)

UNDP, http://magnet.UNDP.org

World Bank, 1994. *Governance: The World Bank's Experience.*

World Bank, 2013. *Social Accountability and Demand for Good Governance*, August 15, (Available at http://www.worldbank.org/en/topic/socialdevelopment/brief/social-accountability)

World Bank, *What is Governance?*(Available at http://web.worldbank.org/WBSITE/EXTERNAL/COUNTRIES/MENAEXT/EXTMNAREGTOPGOVERNANCE/0,contentMDK:20513159~pagePK: 34004173~piPK: 34003707~theSitePK:497024,00.html)

6

Towards Good Governance in India

The Need for Inclusiveness

Leela D'Souza

Introduction

The massive mandate won by Prime Minister Narendra Modi in Uttar Pradesh in the February-March 2017 Assembly Elections, raises a series of questions. The main question according to me is that in the absence of a viable opposition, in a democratic structure like India, what can/will it lead to? It is commonly known that power corrupts and that total power tends to totally corrupt. Humans do not seem be able to handle power, in ways that lead to equality and justice for all. Thus in the absence of a healthy and viable democracy, we need an alternative structure/system. In this case I suggest the importance and relevance of an active and involved civil society, to ensure that democratic goals and values are maintained. But first, let us look at the issue at hand. What is Good Governance?

What is Good Governance?

The *Oxford English Dictionary* defines Governance as, "the act or manner of governing, of exercising control or authority over the actions of subjects; a system of regulations". the *International Encyclopaedia of Social Sciences* has no entry for 'governance'. Perhaps the widest definition of governance is given in the Report of the Commission on Global Governance: "Governance is the sum of the many ways individuals and institutions, public and private, manage their common affairs. It is a continuing process through which conflicting or diverse interests may be accommodated and co-operative action may be taken".[1]

Good governance is an intermediate term, used in international development literature, to describe how public institutions conduct public affairs and manage public resources. According to the International Monetary Fund, Good Governance is implementing the rule of law, improving efficiency and accountability of the public sector, tackling corruption, as essential elements of a framework within which economies can prosper.[2] Too much or too little regulation is not effective. According to the former United Nations Secretary-General, Kofi Annan, "Good governance is ensuring respect for human rights and the rule of law, strengthening democracy, promoting transparency and capacity in public administration. To implement this, the UN suggests eight characteristics. One of the characteristics listed is Effectiveness and Efficiency, where accountability, transparency, equitableness and inclusiveness are the norms to be followed. This requires improving localisation and human rights. Other characteristics include Consensus orientation—to solve conflicts/confrontations between citizens; a Participatory approach, where citizens in various serious and constructive state affairs are involved; and the Rule of Law, where all decisions should follow the common law of the state."[3]

The concept of "Good Governance" often emerges as a model to compare the ineffective economies or political bodies, with viable economies or political bodies. The concept centres on the responsibility of governments and governing bodies to meet the needs of the masses, as opposed to the needs of select groups in the society. Because countries often described as 'most successful' are western, liberal, democratic states, concentrated in Europe and America, good governance standards often measure other state institutions against these states.[4]

Among different cultures, the need and demand for reform can vary, depending on the priorities of that country/society. Because concepts such as civil society and decentralisation, peaceful conflict management and accountability are often used in defining the concept of 'Good governance', it is often closely linked with a democratic Government. However, in 2011, in a study by Alina Rocha Menocal of the Overseas Development Institute, the inconclusiveness of evidence of this relationship is stressed.[5]

Paul Streeten also shows that while freedom and democracy are consistent with good governance and development, they are not tied together in an easy, straightforward, 'functional' way. That civil society and civic culture, as it has evolved over the years, are particularly important for good governance is shown by Robert D. Putnam's excellent book, '*Making Democracy Work*'. He shows that what he calls civic "norms and networks of social engagement", facilitate the working of democracy. the social capital of trust and reciprocity that is invested in norms and networks of civic life is seen as a vital factor of effective government and economic progress. That the market is an important institution of governance is accepted today. Cultural factors also determine and are determined by good governance. Participation of different dimensions of civil society—NGOs, churches, professional organizations, interest groups—although they do not wield ultimate authority—can commit their members to participating in good governance. Both vertical participation and horizontal participation are required.[6]

Good governance does not and cannot take place in a vacuum. It emerges only in the context of existing cultures, the historical development of nations and the existing diversities within societies. And so, the background of a nation, its emerging needs, its progress and its goals for future development, as also its inherent problems and weaknesses, need to be taken into account, before good governance can result. Good governance emerges in being aware of historical realities, answering these needs/overcoming these difficulties. In a country like India, maintaining democratic values is essential; taking all sections of society along in cooperation, not in dominance.

The Historical Reality of India

Before we seek to look into the issue of good governance, we may briefly reflect on the historical reality of India and its inbuilt diversities, which we need to be aware of, so that the democratic process towards good governance is ensured. We need to remember that the national spirit in India was formed as a result of the struggle for Independence against the colonial power. Diverse communities came together for this single purpose. Once India gained freedom and emerged as a nation, the 'fault-lines' on which the nation was formed began manifesting themselves. the term 'fault-lines' include religious, ethnic, language and regional diversities, including tribal and caste distinctions.

The Basis of Diversity in India

The process of forming regions and ethnicities into nations, which began in Europe in the eighteenth century, reached India in the nineteenth century.[7] It was within the context of colonialism that a national sentiment and a sense of patriotism developed in India. Before this period, as Majumdar observes, politically speaking there was no India at the beginning of the nineteenth century.[8] The constant invasions by Greeks, Scythians, Parthians, Huns, Arabs, Turks in the pre-medieval and medieval periods, politically fragmented India.[9] India was in this state of political weakness and confusion, when the Mughal dynasty took control of much of northern India, followed by their defeat to the Western colonial powers—the Dutch, the French, and the British. The Portuguese wrested Goa from Adil Shah of Bijapur in 1513 and Goa was made its capital from 1530, till Goa was liberated by the Indian Army in 1961.[10] Underlying all these developments, we need to understand that the invading powers played into the antagonisms and distrust between the different ruling kingdoms and peoples of India, in order to consolidate their control over the land. Even later, they played one community against the other, in order to maintain their dominance. This process of playing one community against the other or one tribe against the other continues even today in India, especially in the political process, clearly evident during the 2017 Assembly Elections in Uttar Pradesh, where an appeal was made mainly to the OBCs, excluding the Yadavas who were being supported by the Samajwadi Party; and to the Dalits, excluding the Jatava Dalits who were being supported by the Bahujan Samaj Party.

The Struggle for Independence within a Religious Identity

It was within the struggle for Independence from colonial rule, that the spirit of nationalism was born. This struggle, however, took place largely in the realm of a separate religious identity, different from the superiority in the socio-economic realm of the ruling colonial powers. Since in material terms, the West was dominant and providing the format in terms of governance, education and technology, the national culture during Independence was being defined/established largely in terms of the spiritual. As P. Chatterjee, K.N. Panikkar and de Barry observe that the early manifestation of this consciousness of a national spirit was not necessarily in the realm of politics and governance, but found its initial expression in the realm of ideology and culture.[11]

During the struggle for Independence, political mistrust between the Hindus and the Muslims existed, as seen from the fact that no Muslim was on any political organisation or committee. Rather, as soon as the Muslims became politically conscious, they started separate organisations of their own, from 1856 onwards. The differences between the two communities became more pronounced when legislation for local self-government was introduced on an elective basis and the Muslims demanded separate representation as a minority community.[12] This led to the subsequent formation of the Muslim League in 1906. A. Pangariya, Professor of Economics at the Columbia University argues that Nehru's conception of a united, integrated, democratic India, representing all communities and that of Jinnah, who was fighting for the interests of a single community, created a deep gulf between the two perspectives of the Congress Party and the Muslim League, which finally led to Partition.[13]

During the freedom struggle in India, two sharp divergent views had emerged: one as expressed by the secular, democratic, inclusive forces, headed by the Congress under Pandit Jawaharlal Nehru and the other as expressed by the non-secular, communal, exclusivist camp, represented by the Rashtriya Swayamsevak Sangh (RSS) and its ideologues. The formation of the right-wing, Hindu political party, the Hindu Mahasabha in 1915, indicated the coming together of politics and religion. They were giving a call for a religious basis for nationalism. the rise of religious nationalism has thus contributed directly to the rise of religious communalism; the idea of Hindu nationalism being constructed between the years 1870-1920. Religion was thus sought to be made the basis for the emerging identity of India as an end in itself, and not just the basis of the political struggle for freedom, as a means to an end. Such demands for the homogenisation of the Indian identity, led to a feeling of insecurity among the minority communities of India.

No doubt the idea of a two-nation theory was encouraged, even supported by the departing British Government, but the fact remains that India has not been able to resolve the hardening of differences, arising between the Hindu majority and the Muslim minority.

Communal violence in India continues, which is today based not only on religious communalism but also on other criteria—caste, ethnic, language and regional factors.[14]

The Period of Independence

The Founding Fathers of the Constitution of India, being aware of the variety and heterogeneity in our society and its potential for conflict, defined the Indian nation in pluralistic terms, granting equal rights to all its citizens. Embree had observed that national unity can become a code phrase, to denigrate legitimate assertions of cultural pluralism. to understand the complexity of the situation of the Muslim minority in India, it is necessary to keep in mind that during the struggle for Independence, the argument that national identity transcends religious identity, was a basic element in the ideology of the Indian National Congress. Nehru stressed that the democratic process would be involved in building the new society and political order, and this would overcome divisive religious forces.[15]

The initial turbulent years of India as a nation saw no major issues of communal violence. Pandit Nehru, with his emphasis on 'unity in diversity', his astute leadership and a strongly emphasized secular, democratic, inclusive basis for India, managed to steer India on the path of economic growth and development through Five Year Plans, the Green Revolution, Panchayat Raj, Tribal Development and so on. Many of the controversies that emerged in this early period were settled without too much conflict, except perhaps the demands of the South for a separate *Dravidistan,* on the basis of resentment of imposition of Hindi as the national language. Other dissenting issues like the Privy Purse and the re-organisation of States on the basis of ethnic/language/cultural lines were managed effectively.

However, the claim by the opposition of the constant appeasement of the minority Muslim community by the Congress, led to a perceived threat by the majority Hindu community. The decades of the 1980s and the 1990s, saw the emergence of a powerful right wing Hindu movement in India. In 1980, the Jan Sangh changed its name to the Bharatiya Janata Party (BJP) and in 1984, the Bajrang Dal, a militant wing of the Vishwa Hindu Parishad (VHP) was formed. In the 1984 general elections, the BJP won just two seats, but five years later, it won 86 seats. In 1990, the BJP pursued its old demand, (first politically exploited by the Hindu Mahasabha in the 1850s and reactivated in

1949), to construct a *Mandir* (temple) at Ayodhya, on the site where Babur had constructed a mosque in 1528. The destruction of the Babri Masjid at Ayodhya on December 6, 1992, on the basis of the Hindutva ideology, once again ignited fears in the Muslim community and resulted in communal violence. This was followed, between 9 and 12 January, 1993 by organised attacks against the Muslim community in Mumbai, resulting in the bomb blasts in Mumbai in 1993. The continuing expression of Hindutva politics in the following years and the carnage in Gujarat, subsequent to the burning of the train at Godhra, only led to the hardening of the communal divide between Hindus and Muslims.[16]

Other Communal Issues

1. *Sikh Separatism*: The continuing, though watered down demand for a separate, sovereign, Sikh nation, which began as early as the 1920s, and was continued during the struggle for Independence by the Akali Dal, resulted in the formation in 1966 of a separate State for the Sikhs. Sikh Punjabis were in a majority with about 54 per cent of the population of the State, with Hindu Punjabis forming only 44 per cent of the population. The demands for an independent nation continued in the 1980s by Sikh extremists like Harcharan Singh Longowal (1981), and later by Jarnail Singh Bhindranwale (1983). In 1984, Operation Bluestar sought to curb the violent movement. today, the extremist elements in the Sikh leadership have been silenced, with both the SGPC (Shiromani Gurudwara Prabandhak Committee) and the Akali Dal (formed on 14 December, 1920 as the task force of the SGPC, the Sikh religious body), enjoying electoral control in the State. Today the Sikhs have begun to recognise themselves as an integral part of India. Post-2017 Assembly elections, the Congress is back in power in the State.[17]

2. *OBC Caste identity*: Granting of reservations to certain categories has become a contentious issue, which was rendered more severe during the V.P. Singh Government and the implementation of the Mandal Commission recommendations. The proposals of the Mandal Commission (constituted in 1978) and implemented in 1990 by the Government led by V.P. Singh, gave power to the Other Backward Castes (OBCs) and middle level castes. 'Mandalisation' encouraged the OBCs to fight for a separate electoral space and a share in governance, resulting in the creation of new ethnic and caste groups, forming political parties to contest elections in States, as has happened in Uttar Pradesh, Bihar, Odisha, Tamil Nadu and other States. New majority-minority conflicts have arisen, with the tendency of the newly formed political parties to politicise issues on the basis of religion, ethnicity, caste and language, causing new bases of tension (this was clearly in evidence in the Assembly elections in Uttar Pradesh in 2017).

3. ***North East India: Tribal Identity***: In the North eastern States, separate tribal groups have not managed to form an electoral alliance, and much struggle is still taking place for the supremacy of one tribe over the other. At Independence, the political boundaries of the North East were arbitrarily drawn, leaving uncertain grey zones, disputed territories and discontented peoples, demanding various degrees of autonomy or independence. In response to the demands of the different dominant tribes, the North East region of India is carved out into seven separate States. But still there is no peace in that region and there is a constant insurgency by local tribal groups demanding separate recognition, as for example Bodoland and more recently a modified Nagaland State. Regionalism is thus taking on more complicated forms, where the earlier call for Indian nationalism has now transferred itself to ethno-nationalism.[18]

The Current Situation

The Challenge for Jobs

The BJP Government has won a landslide victory in the 2017 Assembly elections in Uttar Pradesh (U.P.), giving Mr. Modi unprecedented potential to implement economic and social policies, to initiate economic growth and to establish social equality among all sections of the people. It was on the platform of inclusive growth and development, as also the message of Hindutva that he largely won in U.P. But as a former RSS *Pracharak,* Modi is unable to rid himself of the Hindutva ideology hardliners. But can the Hindutva ideology deliver development, seeing that it is not based on inclusiveness? In the U.P. Assembly elections, Mr. Modi reached out to the non-Yadav OBCs and the non-Jatav Dalit castes, but the composition of the U.P. Assembly does not reflect this inclusion; greater representation (44%) is given to the upper castes (Brahmin, Rajput, Bania, Bhumihar, Kayastha), followed by the OBCs (33%)

Kurmi, Jat, Lodh, Gujjar, Kushwaha (no Yadavas), and a smaller representation to the SCs, STs, and others One seat is given to a Muslim.[19] The key challenge for development and inclusive growth in job creation. In spite of Modi's "Hindutva plus development" model in Gujarat for twelve years, reports show that Gujarat still suffers from large scale unemployment. As academic Pranab Bardhwan explains, "Gujarat welcomed capital intensive, petro-chemical and pharma sectors that did not provide jobs for the uneducated and semi-skilled workers."[20]

Respecting Religious Diversity

The purpose of the Fundamental Rights in the Constitution is to preserve individual liberty and democratic principles, based on equality to all members of the society. But the Hindutva model of governance relies on State control of the citizen. The State is playing a crucial role in the propagation of Hindutva, an exclusionary ideology, with little space for individual rights and free will. The liberalisation in 1991 showed that rolling back of powers of the State is required to achieve high growth, not asserting State power.[21]

The shutting down of alleged 'illegal' slaughterhouses in U.P., (and other BJP ruled States),[22] under Chief Minister Yogi Adityanath, speaks volumes. Even licensed slaughterhouses and export-oriented units are reported to have been closed down on flimsy grounds. Fauzan Alavi, Secretary, All India Meat and Livestock Exporters Association said that the meat industry is valued at Rs. 50,000 crore and provided employment to five lakh people, of which only 25 (twenty-five) per cent were Muslims, the rest being Hindus, mostly OBCs. U.P. accounts for sixty per cent of India's trade meat and dairy products. In fact, the meat industry is a by-product of the dairy business. Farmers are now allowing their unproductive cows to wander, while unproductive buffaloes are sold to slaughter houses. Thus rearing cows is becoming economically unviable. Dairy products will also soon get affected in a trickle-down impact.[23] Soon the leather and footwear industries may also get impacted. There is much uncertainty about the future.

Incidentally, the recitation of '*Vande Mataram*' is made compulsory before entering the Assembly Hall. It is felt that respecting the sentiments of the 'others' in a society with intense religious diversity, is very essential for maintaining communal harmony and peaceful co-existence.

Creating Other Centres of Authority

In a representative democracy like India, the electorate votes/elects into power, but political power is then exercised indirectly through the elected representatives. Today, however, when no viable opposition exists, other centres of authority can be created—like civil society, i.e. the ruling political party need not be the only centre of authority. Civic bodies can be given power to operate in certain social and civic areas, to ensure inclusiveness in implementing social and economic policies/plans. This will lead to a more participatory democracy.

Revival of the Co-operative System

We feel that there is a need for a greater revival of the Co-operative system, especially in rural areas. The extreme success of the milk co-operative, under the able leadership of Dr. Kurian, is a case in point. Here the catch word is good governance; capable, honest and transparent leadership where the benefits reach the grassroots and are not siphoned off by vested interests. Unfortunately, the sugar co-operatives in Maharashtra are largely under the dominant control of one person/party. They control large tracts of land and are the main beneficiaries of the profits of the sugar co-operative.

Leadership by Non-Political Personnel

Co-operatives can operate at a dual level. One, as the basis for greater participation of the people, to ensure that the benefits of Government policies reach the people and are not swallowed up by middlemen; two, they can ensure inclusive growth, where each category of skilled workers in rural India form co-operatives, to ensure that the traditional skills are not lost, but are improved with new technologies. Even agricultural and meat products can also be brought under co-operatives. Issues like loans, profitable marketing of the goods, increasing the scope of production etc., can be managed by each co-operative, where the people themselves can take responsibility for their own success and new innovations, under the guidance of able leadership.

What is required is a good and honest leadership by non-political personnel, who are honest, capable and exhibit transparency in their dealings, to ensure that the benefits of government schemes reach the people. It is well known that in India much of the funds allociated for specific projects intended to benefit the poor and needy sections of the society do not reach them, but are siphoned off by middle men. the same holds true of financial assistance sanctioned during natural calamities. Good governance is required to ensure that all those who are intended to benefit, do so. Here civil society and even NGOs can play a prominent role, working with and through the local Panchayats and/or cooperative societies. The underlying need is personal integrity and honesty.

In spite of the best efforts by the Government to ensure that all sections of society benefit, we often find that even the NGOs and other bodies who volunteer to assist in times of natural calamities, operate like the former middle men, where large amounts of cash and other benefits are retained by the group in charge. It demands the strength and integrity of the person organising the NGO to ensure that the benefits are not usurped. Modi's genuine intentions to allow benefits to reach directly to the beneficiaries through bank transactions are yet to become fully operational.

Conclusion

Ensuring inclusive growth in India is not easy, given the deep religious, class and caste divide, both in rural as well as urban sections. Gandhiji had observed that if rural India progresses, India will develop. The focus needs to be on bringing rural India under good governance and including them in economic and social development. Other underlying problems in India, like population increase, will be automatically addressed, when economic development takes place, leading to the demand for education and higher education for their children.

Former U.S. President, Barack Obama once observed, regarding Nigeria, that no amount of economic aid or oil would ensure progress, without Good governance.[24]

Notes

1. Streeton, Paul, *Good Governance: History and Development of the Concept* (Available at https://www.upscsuccess.com/sites/default/files/documents/Good%20governance%20History%20and% 20development% 20).

2. *See*, https://en.wikipedia.org/wiki/Good_governance.
3. *See*, https://en.wikipedia.org/wiki/good governance.
4. *See*, https://en.wikipedia.org/wiki/Good_governance.
5. *See*, https://en.wikipedia.org/wiki/good governance.
6. Streeten, Paul. *op. cit.*
7. This idea has been discussed more extensively in D'Souza, Leela. (2002), "Ethnic Nationalism in India – An Appraisal" in *Vidyajyoti Journal* of *Theological Reflection* (VJTR), Vol. 66, No. 1, January, pp. 36-37.
8. Majumdar, R.C., (1965), (a) "Growth of Political Ideas and Political Organization (Upto 1858)", pp. 432; (b) "Indian People at the Beginning of the Nineteenth Century", pp. 4; (c). "Birth of Nationalism", p. 465. In R.C. Majumdar (Gen. Ed). The *History and Culture of the Indian People. British Paramountcy and Indian Renaissance Part II.* Bombay : Bharatiya Vidya Bhavan.
9. The purity of the people east of the Indus river was initially dissolved in the post-Harappan period, with the migration of the successive waves of the Aryan-speaking people and the subsequent 'Dasarajna war' or the Battle of the Ten Kings. See Leela D'Souza, (2007), *Cultural History of Ancient India. Diversity, Syncretism, Synthesis.* Jaipur/New Delhi : Rawat Publications, pp. 145-148.
10. D'Souza, Leela. (2007), "St. Francis Xavier and the Jesuits in Goa. The Socio-Political Context" in Delio de Mendonca (Ed.). *Jesuits in India. History and Culture.* Goa : Xavier Centre of Historical Research and Gujarat, Gujarat Sahitya Prakash, pp. 38-39.
11. Chatterjee, P. (1986), *Nationalist Thought* and the *Colonial World. A Derivative Discourse.* New Delhi (1986). Oxford University Press, p. 2; T. deBary, *et al.* (Compilers), (1991), *Sources of Indian Tradition*, Vol. II. Edited and revised by Stephen Hay, Delhi: Viking. p. 276; K.N. Panikkar, (1995), *Culture, Ideology and Hegemony. Intellectuals and Social Consciousness in Colonial India,* New Delhi (1995) Tulika. p. 57. Leela D'Souza, *Vidyajyoti Journal of Theological Reflection*, *op. cit.*, pp. 38-39.
12. Majumdar, R.C. (1965), "Muslim Community", pp. 297, 302, in R.C. Majumdar (Gen. Ed.) *op. cit.*
13. Panagariya, A. (2009), "Some Questions are Best Buried", in *Times of India*, October, 31, p. 16; Leela D'Souza, "Communal Violence and Assertion of Identity" in *Social Action*, 2010. Vol. 60, January-March. p. 16.
14. D'Souza, Leela, *Social Action, op. cit.*, pp. 15-17.
15. Embree, A.T. (1992), *Utopias* in *Conflict. Religion and Nationalism in Modern India*. Delhi : Oxford University Press, pp. 77-78; Leela D'Souza, (2011), "Cultural Pluralism and Nation Building. The need to Reconstruct Identities" in *Indian Journal of Secularism*, Vol. 14, No. 4, January– March, p. 54.
16. D'Souza, Leela, Social Action, *op. cit.*, pp. 17-18.
17. Kapur, R.A. (1986), *Sikh Separatism. The Politics of Faith*. London. Allen & Unwin Publishers Ltd., pp. 216, 219-236. Leela D'Souza, *Social Action.*

op. cit., pp. 18-19.

18. Pandey, G. and Yunus Samad (2007), *Fault-lines of Nationhood*. Delhi: Lotus Collection. Roli Books. pp. 56-57; M.S. Prabhakara (2007), "Ethno-Nationalism: Theory and Practice" in *The Hindu*, October 28, p. 8. Leela D'Souza. *Social Action*. *op. cit.*, pp. 20-21.
19. Trivedi Centre for Political Data. Ashok University, Sonepat, Haryana. Accessed at https://scroll.in/article/831675/uttar-pradesh-2017-these-charts-examine-the-surge-in-indias-heartland.
20. Sagarika Ghose (2017), "Can Hindutva deliver Vikas?" in *Times of India*. March 29, p. 18.
21. *Ibid.*
22. *Times News Network*, "Four BJP Governments swoop down on illegal meat shops", in *Times of India*, 2017, March 29, p. 10.
23. Alavi, Fauzan, Secretary, All India Meat and Livestock Exporters Association (AIMLEA), in an interview with Subhash Mishra, "Meat Exporters feel they are not doing business, but committing a crime – officials closing slaughterhouses on flimsy reasons", in *Times of India*, 2017, March 29, p. 18.
24. https://en.wikipedia.org/wiki/good governance.

7

Policies for Tribal Communities in India

Continuity from Pre-Independence to Post-Independence Period

John Solomon Gaikwad

Introduction

The term *'tribe'* was adapted by Anthropologists from ordinary usage in English. In Medieval English the word *'tribe'* indicated "a primary aggregate of people claiming descent from a common ancestor". With the advent of colonization, European Anthropologists applied the term *'tribe'* to people who lived in a primitive condition in backward areas and did not know the use of writing. Since then the term *'tribe'* has been widely *accepted* and has been operational as a technical/academic/administrative term to denote the *aborigines. The 'tribal'* population is also termed as *native/indigenous* population in Anthropological literature. Tribal society is often referred to as *primitive society/pre-state society/folk-society.*

India has the largest concentration of tribal population in the world next only to the African Continent. There are more than 500 tribal communities in India (Verma, 1990). In the Indian context, the tribal communities are termed as *adivasi/vanya-jati/jana-jati/jana-jamaty.* The habitat of most of the tribal communities is forests, hills, plateaus situated in deep interior and isolated regions.

Tribal communities have been an integral part of the Indian society and have always co-existed with the general masses/non-tribal people and lived in the close vicinity for centuries. Circumstances often drove the tribal people to the quiet corners of the country. After being absolutely cut off from the mainstream, the tribal communities became losers and sufferers due to exploitation by the powerful and dominant ruling class. This ultimately led the tribal communities to be overburdened with misery and distress. As a result of the confinement, each tribal community achieved a degree of equilibrium with their ecology and reduced to a state of utter ignorance. Each of the isolated tribal communities developed a specific way of life with a set of typical thought and behaviour pattern. These isolated tribal communities were considered to be happy enough in their own world.

Administration During British Period

The British, who were primarily concerned with the non-tribal population on the mainland, decided to *keep away* the isolated, forest dwelling tribal communities from the day-to-day administration. Most of the tribal areas were under/adjoining the territories of indigenous rulers/*zamindars* (land-lords).[1&2]

The powerful *zamindars* began to exploit the tribal people and conspiring with the corrupt officials, forced the tribal people to vacate the lands in their possession. Also, taking advantage of the helpless condition of the tribals, the traders and money-lenders took every opportunity to exploit them. In this process, the tribal communities completely lost their age-old rights on land. With this, the traditional economy of the tribal communities was challenged. As a result of overall exploitation of the isolated, forest dwelling tribal communities, there was a great discontent among them. The tribal communities began to launch violent revolts and militant struggle in different tribal areas.[3]

Based on the recommendations of a German expert, Dr. Voelcker, the British Government introduced the Indian Forest Act, 1894. This was another reason for the agitation of the tribal communities because according to this Act, their traditional rights on forests were no longer recognised by the British Government. This Act severely affected the tribal life, economy and culture. With this law, the tribals became *'trespassers'* in their age-old habitat. Their free movement inside the forests was legally restricted. As a result of forceful displacement from the forests, *their homes,* there was a strong discontent among the isolated, forest dwelling tribal communities. The disturbed tribal communities resorted to non-cooperation with the British Government. Violent revolts and militant struggles were resorted to by many tribal communities. In handling such revolts, the British

Government resorted to ruthless executive and legislative measures. The British Government introduced the Criminal Tribes Act, 1871. According to this Act, 153 tribal communities in different parts of India were branded as Criminal tribes.

The Government decided to specify tribal areas as Scheduled Tracts under the Scheduled District Act, 1874. The main objective of this Act was to exclude the specified areas from the day-to-day administrative operations under the ordinary laws. According to the British Government, such a segregation of the tribal communities into specified areas was necessary for their protection from severe exploitation by outsiders.

"The Government of India Act, 1919 empowered the Governor General in Council to declare 'Scheduled Tracts', on the recommendation from the Secretary of State. The identified 'Scheduled Tracts' were classified as *Wholly Excluded Areas* and *Partially Excluded Areas.* The Governor had all the Legislative powers over the Wholly Excluded Areas. The frontier and border regions in Assam, Laccadive and Minicoy Islands (then in the Province of Madras), Chittagong hill tracts (of Bengal), Lahul (in Himachal Pradesh), Spiti (in Punjab), Angul (in Orissa) etc. were declared as *wholly excluded Areas.* Extensive tribal tracts in the provinces of Bihar, Bengal, Orissa, Uttar-Pradesh, Madhya Pradesh, Bombay and Madras were declared as *Partially Excluded Areas.*

Based on the recommendations of Simon Commission (1929), the Government of India Act, 1935 was introduced with special provisions for the special treatment of the tribal areas. According to this Act, the *Wholly Excluded Areas* were placed under the Provincial rule of the Governor and the *Partially Excluded Areas* were placed within the fold of Ministerial responsibility.

Hence, exclusion was the main policy of the British Government. By virtue of these arrangements, the British Government succeeded in keeping the tribal communities *isolated* from the mainstream national life. Many leaders, activists and academicians have observed that the main objective of the British Government's *isolation* of the tribal communities from the mainstream of national life was to keep them *far away* from the freedom movement. The British Government considered the tribal communities to be hostile towards their administration. Hence, the tribal areas were cut off from the civil administration. The British Government was completely indifferent towards safeguarding the interests of the tribal communities. The non-intervention policy of the British Government was known as *Laissez faire*. Neglect of tribal communities by the British Government subjected the helpless tribals to ruthless exploitation by traders, moneylenders, landlords, contractors and corrupt officials. However, as the British Government never objected to any of the traditional customs of the tribal communities, they could retain their customs, traditions, language and culture.

Post-Independence Period

After attaining Independence, the Republic of India undertook the dual challenge of complete reconstruction of the nation to fulfil the needs and aspirations of all the citizens. Inorder to achieve this goal, India became *a welfare state* and resorted to the path of planned development. At the time of independence, all the State Governments and the Central Government were aware that the tribal communities are most vulnerable and the weakest of weaker sections in the society.

Important Constitutional Safeguards for Tribal Communities

The Constitution of India has made specific provisions for tribal communities, inorder to safeguard their rights and interests as citizens of independent India. Thus, Article 342 of the Constitutional Order, 1950, empowers the President of India to notify the *most deprived tribes* in consultation with different State Governments. Accordingly, 559 tribes located in 14 States (in 1950), were declared as Scheduled Tribes. Article 366 (25) designates such *deprived tribes* as *Scheduled Tribes*.

Fifth Schedule (Part VI of Article 244)

This is a special provision for Scheduled Tribe communities. the Fifth Schedule to the Constitution is the charter of Scheduled Areas and Scheduled Tribes. The President of India is empowered to declare any under-developed area, having substantial population of Scheduled Tribes, as Scheduled Areas. the Governors of the states having Scheduled Areas are given special powers over such areas, despite the fact that these areas are administered as a part of the state, where these are located. The Governors are required to prepare Reports of the Administration of Scheduled Areas, for submission to the President of India. The President of India directs each state having Scheduled Areas, to constitute a Tribes Advisory Council, to advise on matters pertaining to the advancement and development of the Scheduled Tribes in the state. [Scheduled Areas under Fifth Schedule were formerly Partially Excluded Areas].

Sixth Schedule (Part VI of Article 244)

The Sixth Schedule to the Constitution deals with the administration of Assam (as in 1950), in following two zones:

- The autonomous Districts including United *Khasi-Jaintia* Hills District, the *Garo* Hills District, the *Mizo* District, the North *Cachar* Hills, District and the *Mikir* Hills District.
- The North East Frontier Agency comprising the North-Eastern Frontier Tract including *Balipara* Frontier tract, *Tirap* Frontier Tract, *Abor* Hills District and *Misinic* Hills District.

This Schedule advocates for the setting up of a District Council in each autonomous District and a Regional Council in each autonomous region. These Councils have been given special powers.

The Criminal Tribes: De-Notified, 1952

After Independence, the Criminal Tribes Act, 1871 was repealed in 1952, resulting in 153 communities branded as criminals by the British Government being *de-notified.* Hence, with an encouraging and a positive action taken by the Government, the *de-notified* communities got rid of the social stigma of criminality.

Policy on Tribal Development: Arriving at a Consensus

After Independence, various policies for tribal development were discussed. These include:

1. Policy of Segregation

This policy was similar to the policy of *isolation* adopted by the British Government. Verrier Elvin and Christoph Von Furer-Haimendorf advocated that the tribal communities practicing *animism* were *quite different* from the followers of Hinduism and that they should be allowed to conserve the distinct features of their traditions and culture. Verrier Elwin, who was a member of the NEFA Administration, had recommended *temporary isolation,* of tribal communities in certain specific circumstances.

In the light of the *Laissez faire* policy of the British, the policy of segregation was severely opposed by the nationalist leaders in India, who criticised the policy of isolation as a *negative approach of seclusion.* Ram Manohar Lohia and G.S. Ghurye strongly condemned the policy of segregation. It was advocated that segregation cannot be permanent policy because isolation would never lead to progress and advancement. It was pointed out that the aborigines of Australia, *Arya* speaking *Khalar* and *Kati* tribes from Rampur Valley of *Chitral* have clearly indicated that isolation ultimately leads to stagnation and death. Later Verrier Elwin stated that *our policy was neither to isolate the tribes, nor to freeze their culture and way of life as it is.* Jawaharlal Nehru described this policy as a *'closed door'* policy, adopted by the colonial government to protect the distinctive and colourful life of the tribal communities in isolated pockets.[4]

2. Policy of Assimilation

As opposed to the policy of Segregation, Dr. G.S. Ghurye, advocated a policy of Assimilation on the grounds that these extremely backward tribal communities need not be treated as aborigines as they belonged to the fold of Hinduism. According to him, complete assimilation in Hindu society was the best solution for solving the problems of the tribal communities. It was indicated that acceptance of policy of assimilation of the tribal people, would lead to forcing the tribal communities to completely forget their customs, traditions, language/dialects and culture, in order to assimilate with, and adopt the culture of the people in the main-stream. In India, complete assimilation of tribal communities will not be possible without violating their own culture. This approach had a potential danger of chaotic/violent reactions of the tribal communities, if they are forced to *give up/forget their own culture in order to adopt an alien culture.* Such violent reactions, as a result of forceful assimilation have been observed among the tribal communities of Australia, Melanesia and the USA.

Dr. N.K. Bose opined that *the policy of complete assimilation was against humanity.* He observed that *the culture contact and borrowing of cultural traits for centuries could not transform heterogeneous Indian society into a single homogenous society.* He indicated that a policy of *limited assimilation* could be useful in the Indian context. Jawaharlal Nehru described this policy as the *open door* policy; an approach advocated by social workers. With this approach, the tribal communities would be exposed to different external influences.

3. Policy of Integration

From the above debate it would be observed that the first two policies proposed (segregation and assimilation), were two extreme points on a continuum. Moreover, the policy for tribal development was most explicitly outlined by Jawaharlal Nehru. He could not absolutely support either of the first two policies, namely the *segregation/ isolation — closed door* and the *assimilation/limited isolation — open door.* Nehru wanted a policy which would help the tribal communities to be integrated into the larger society without losing their distinctive identity. the political leaders, nationalist leaders, academicians, social activists, social workers and administrators reached a consensus and agreed to adopt the rational policy proposed by Jawaharlal Nehru. This widely appreciated and accepted policy of *integration* was amid-way between the two extreme points on the continuum. The approach of integrating tribal communities with the mainstream was believed to be useful for bringing the tribal communities *at the same level,* with the rest of the population. It was indicated that the policy of integration would encourage the preservation of traditions, customs, practices, languages/dialects and culture of the tribal communities. This would ensure that the fundamental basis of tribal life would not be disturbed. While the tribal communities were encouraged to preserve their culture, they were free to borrow and incorporate new traits, in their way of life. It was believed that the policy of integration would be instrumental in the prevention of exploitation of the tribal communities, while they enjoy equal rights and opportunities in a developing society.

'Panch Sheel' of Tribal Development

In 1959, Jawaharlal Nehru proposed a set of five principles, the *Panch Sheel,* for the development of tribal communities in his *foreword* to the book, *A Philosophy for NEFA,* by Verrier Elwin. This policy constitutes an important milestone in the domain of tribal development. The *'Panch Sheel'* for tribal development included:

1. Development along the lines of their own genius and avoidance of imposing anything on them. Their own traditional arts and culture should be encouraged;
2. Tribal rights in lands and forests should be respected;
3. Train and build a team of their own people to handle administration and development. Some technical personnel from outside will, no doubt, are needed, especially in the beginning. Avoid introducing too many outsiders into tribal territory;
4. There should not be an over-administration of tribal areas or overwhelming them with the multiplicity of schemes. One should work through and not in rivalry to their own social and cultural institutions; and
5. Results should be judged not by statistics or the amount of money spent, but by the quality of human character that is evolved.

Panch Sheel: Some Reflections

Jawaharlal Nehru advocated the need for *psychological approach* for achieving psychological integration (A New Deal for Tribal India: Report of the Scheduled Areas and Scheduled Tribes Commissions, 1963, quoted in Mathur H.M.—1977:489-90). His love for the tribal communities found expression in his efforts to mix with them as frequently as possible, to show friendly and familiar gesture...and safeguard their interests (Vidyarthi, 1968). Addressing an All India Conference of the tribal communities held at Jagdalpur in March 1955, Nehru advised his tribal brethren in the following words:

> "Wherever you live, you should live in your own way. This is what I want you to decide yourselves, how you would like to live. Your old customs and habits are good. We want that they should survive; but at the same time we want that you should be educated and should do your part in welfare of our country" (1955:16).

Importance of Education and Communication in Integration

In the North Eastern Frontier Agency (NEFA), Jawaharlal Nehru gave priority to roads and schools and opined that "given these communication and schools, they would advance rapidly and give credit to the country in many ways" (1952-A). In spite of his anxiety to see that the tribal communities become educationally and economically advanced, Nehru always hoped that there would be no attempt made to impose other ways of life on them in a hurry. He advised: *"Let the change come gradually and be worked out by the tribal communities themselves"* (Nehru,1957). Jawaharlal Nehru gave considerable thought to the language problem, which he considered was exceedingly important from the psychological point of view. He made it absolutely clear that the Government would encourage the tribal languages. He stood not only for allowing the tribal languages to continue but made it his policy "to encourage and help them to flourish" (Vidyarthi, 1968). In this matter, he was greatly influenced by Lenin who won the goodwill of the tribal people of the Soviet Union by encouraging their language, by going out of the way in helping hundreds of dialects, by preparing dictionaries and vocabularies and even by evolving new scripts where there were none (Vidyarthi, 1968). Jawaharlal Nehru was convinced that it was a wise policy of Lenin for winning over illiteracy and above all to create an impression on them that they could live their own lives and in the light of this lesson, he advised all of us "to go out of our way to do so in context with Indian Tribal population" (1952).

Other Constitutional Safeguards

Article 46 of the Constitution provides for the protection of weaker sections of the population. Directive Principle (under Article 46), indicates that "the State shall promote with special care the educational and economic interests of the weaker sections of the people, and, in particular of the Scheduled Castes and the Scheduled Tribes, and shall protect them from social injustice and all forms of exploitation."

Article 330, 332 and 334 provide for reservations of seats for Scheduled Tribes in the Legislative Assemblies and the Parliament.

Article 335 has a provision for securing adequate representation and appointments of Scheduled Tribes in services and posts in connection with the affairs of the Union or the States.

Article 16(4) makes a provision for reservation of posts in favour of the Scheduled Tribes.

Articles 15, 19, 23 and 29 provide for safe guarding the Scheduled Tribes against exploitation and protection of their civic rights.

Article 275 provides for Financial Assistance to the States for the Development of Scheduled Areas and Scheduled Tribes in different States.

Article 338 provides for setting up of a National Commission for Scheduled Castes and Scheduled Tribes, which would be consulted by the Union Government and the State Governments on all major policy matters affecting Scheduled Castes and Scheduled Tribes. Finally, Article 339 of the Constitution requires an evaluation of the progress in the domain of the development of the Scheduled Tribes.

Legal Safeguards

Several legislations were introduced to protect the interests of the Scheduled Tribes. Salient features of some important landmark legislations are given below:

Act for Restoration of Agricultural Land Alienated from Tribal Communities, 1976

According to the provisions of this Act, agricultural land alienated from tribal people has to be immediately restored to the tribal individual/family. This step was taken to curb the exploitation of the tribal people by private money-lenders and traders. As per the provisions of this Act:

- All transactions of transfer of agricultural land (belonging to tribal people), in the name of non-tribal individuals were declared to be null and void, with retrospective effect; and
- All such transactions of transfers of agricultural land (belonging to tribal people), in the future will not be allowed in any manner whatsoever.

Act for Improvement of Economic Conditions of Tribal Communities, 1976

This Act is meant to prevent exploitation of the tribal people by private money-lenders and traders. According to the provisions of this Act:

- Money-lending to the tribal people is banned;
- Traders and money-lenders are banned from purchasing agricultural produce and minor forest produce from the tribals;
- State Co-operative Tribal Development Corporation was established in each State having substantial tribal population and each such Corporation was given the responsibility of establishing linkages with Tribal Co-operative Societies established at the village level in tribal areas;
- The Tribal Co-operative Societies were given the responsibility of monopoly procurement/purchase of notified agricultural produce and minor forest produce from the tribals. The rates of procurement were to be notified by the Government, from time to time; and
- The Tribal Co-operative Societies were given the responsibility of providing Consumption Finance to the tribal families at the beginning of the monsoon season. After getting agriculture produce, the repayment of the consumption finance has to be done by selling the agriculture produce/ minor forest produce at the monopoly procurement centre established by the tribal co-operative society.

Law on Panchayati Raj Extension to Scheduled Areas, 1992

The Panchayati Raj (Local Self-Government Institutions System), comprise the following three constituents:

- Gram Panchayat (at the village level);
- Panchayat Samiti (at the Tehsil level); and
- Zilla Parishad (at the District level).

This system was initially launched for development in rural areas. Later on, the provisions of the Panchayati Raj Institutions System were extended to the Scheduled Areas (Tribal Areas), for the implementation of development programmes more effectively at the grassroots level. In the *Panchayati Raj* System, the Gram Sabha (Village Council), comprising the common people is very powerful.

Recognition of Forest Rights of Scheduled Tribes Act, 2006

The Recognition of Forest Rights of Scheduled Tribes Act is a landmark legislation, under which the Government of India in the Ministry of Tribal Affairs has recognized the traditional rights of the forest dwelling tribal communities, for (a) cultivation in the forest areas; and (b) access to community forest resources such as minor water bodies, fishing, non-forest timber produce etc.

Government of India has prescribed an elaborate community-led administrative procedure for recognition of the forest rights of the Scheduled Tribes. The success of this Act lies in the fact that the people at the village level have been given an opportunity to have partnership in the process of management, protection and conservation of the forests.

Recommendation by Commissions and Committees

Being aware of and sensitive to the problems of the tribal communities, the Government of India has appointed various Commissions and Expert Committees from time to time, seeking expert advice for solving the problems associated with tribal development.

The Dhebar Commission

A Scheduled Areas and Scheduled Tribes Commission appointed in 1961, under the Chairmanship of U.N. Dhebar, emphasized the importance of integration of tribal communities. It was stated that the tribal communities being members of the Indian family, the development programmes should aim for the integration of tribal communities. The Dhebar Commission strongly advocated the integration of all the available resources (land, forest, and cattle wealth and cottage/village industries) for the development of the tribal communities. Considering the importance of *'harmony of tribal life'*, it was recommended that nothing should be imposed upon the tribal people. the Commission also strongly recommended the establishment of Tribal Research and Training Institutes in the States having substantial Tribal Population. Accordingly, 15 States have established such Institutes.

P. Shilu Ao Committee

An expert committee headed by Shri P. Shilu Ao (former Chief Minister of Nagaland), indicated that the aim of tribal development should be defined as the progressive socio-economic advancement of the tribal communities. This would help the tribal communities to get integrated with the rest of the community on an equal footing within a reasonable time. About the time factor, the Committee rightly pointed that the time factor will vary from tribe to tribe, depending upon the stage of development of each tribe. It was found that there was a wide divergence in the socio-economic, cultural and technological conditions of the 559 Scheduled Tribes in the country.

Dr. S.C. Dube Committee

An expert committee under the chairmanship of Dr. S.C. Dube, an Anthropologist, was set up in 1972 by the Planning Commission for formulation of a new strategy for tribal development during the Fifth Five-year Plan (1974–1979). Reviewing the situation of the tribal communities, the Committee observed that only 40 per cent of the tribal population could come under the purview of the development programmes. Hence, the Committee recommended a fast and time-bound integrated area development programme suited to the genius of the people. This programme was aimed at elimination of all forms of exploitation in order to move towards the goal of equality and justice.

With this approach of integrated development, the concept of Tribal Sub Plan was adopted during the Fifth Five-Year Plan. It was clear that a uniform prescription was neither possible, nor desirable because with a wide divergence of the cultural fabric, of tribal communities would not respond equally to a master plan.

Dr. C.H. Hanumantha Rao Committee

In 1984, the Planning Commission appointed an expert committee headed by Dr. C.H. Hanumantha Rao, which recommended de-centralisation during the Seventh Five-Year Plan (1985–1990). Accordingly, the Tribal Sub-Plan was extended to all tribal groups of the country. The area oriented developmental programmes were replaced by the *'family oriented'* economic programmes. The families from *below poverty line* were expected to be elevated to *'above the poverty line'*. Different pockets of the country were chosen for the implementation of the programme. Emphasis was laid upon formal and non-formal education, with an expectation that education would generate the necessary confidence among the tribal people, for interacting with non-tribal people. In order to make the plan highly functional, the working committee recommended a blending of the elements of the fifth and sixth schedules.

Tribal Development in the Realm of Planned Development

Independent India became a welfare state and took up the path of planned development; aimed to be achieved through ambitious Five-Year Plans. The Central Planning Commission is assisted by State Planning Boards. Early 1950s witnessed some important structural changes in the administrative system in India. In the beginning, the general administration was assigned the task of development administration. The tribal development programme was taken up during early 1950s and a Tribal Welfare Department was established by the Government of India in 1951. This initiated the establishment of Social/Tribal Welfare Departments in different states.

First Five-Year Plan: 1951-1955

Inorder to achieve an overall development of social, economic and cultural life of the tribal communities, welfare activities were concentrated in the domains of economy, education, health and housing. These special programmes were implemented through the Community Development Blocks in tribal areas and jointly undertaken by the Ministry of Home Affairs and the Ministry of Community Development & Co-operation.

Second Five-Year Plan: 1956-1960

More pervasive approach was planned to be implemented in the most under-developed areas of tribal concentration through the Special Multipurpose Tribal Development Blocks. More facilities were planned for the tribal communities throughout the country. The main emphasis was on economic development through agriculture, cottage industries, forest and co-operative societies.

Third Five-Year Plan: 1961-1965

This Plan adopted a broad strategy of socio-economic development, through Tribal Development Blocks. the development programmes gave priority to economic development, education, health, housing and communication. This Plan adopted an integrated approach to link tribal economy with the National economy.

Fourth Five-Year Plan: 1969-1974

During 1966, 1967 and 1968, Annual Plans were implemented separately every year.

The strategy, programmes and approach remained the same as in case of the Third Five-Year Plan.

Fifth Five-Year Plan: 1974-1979

As per the recommendations of Dr. S.C. Dube Committee, the concept of Tribal Sub-Plan was introduced for Integrated Tribal Development. The Tribal Sub-Plan approach which aimed at an integrated and over all socio-economic development of the tribal communities, kept the following factors in view while preparing Sub-Plan:

- Identification/demarcation of the areas of tribal concentration;
- Identification of socio-cultural barriers;
- Identification of socio-cultural promoters of change in development;
- Assessment of special problems and special needs of the tribal areas;
- Assessment of the resources available for the Sub-Plan;
- Formulation of programmes from various sectors; and
- Suitable infrastructure and administrative set up.

During the Fifth Five-Year Plan period, the Sub-Plan was implemented in different States and Union Territories, covering 63.81 per cent of the total tribal population of the country. Special Multipurpose Tribal Blocks were designated as Tribal Development Blocks. Integrated Tribal Development Projects were launched in Tribal Sub-Plan Areas having "Tribal Development Blocks."

The development programmes since the Fifth Five-Year Plan have been described by various terms such as Tribal Sub-Plan Approach/ Integrated Tribal Development Programme/Area Development

Programme/Problem Solving Approach. These various terms explain the multiple dimensions of the programmes implemented. At the end of the plan period it was observed that an overall development of all the tribal communities could not be achieved.

Sixth Five-Year Plan: 1980-1985

While the Tribal Sub-Plan approach continued, the main thrust of the strategy was shifted to Modified Area Development Approach. Tribal pockets outside the Integrated Tribal Development Projects were included for implementation of development programmes. The criteria for implementation of the development programmes under Integrated Tribal Development Projects included :

- Tribal population in the areas of tribal concentration;
- Dispersed tribal population, outside the ITDPs (Minimum 5000 Tribal population, in a population of 10,000, in a specific region); and
- Primitive Tribal Communities.

During the Sixth Five-Year Plan, 52 communities were identified as primitive tribes in different States and Union Territories. Different types of development programmes were implemented in the three types of areas identified, viz. Area oriented programmes for Tribal population in areas of tribal concentration; Community oriented programmes for Dispersed tribal population outside ITDPs and Individual Family oriented programmes for Primitive Tribal Communities.

Seventh Five-Year Plan: 1985-1990

Tribal Sub-Plan strategy with thrust on Modified Area Development Approach continued. In accordance with the Hanumantha Rao Committee recommendations for decentralisation of the Seventh Five-Year Plan, the Tribal Sub-Plan was extended to all tribal groups of the country. The area-oriented developmental programmes were replaced by the *family oriented* economic programmes. The families from *below poverty line* were expected to be elevated to *above the poverty line.* Different pockets of the country were chosen for the implementation of the programme. Emphasis was laid upon formal and non-formal education, with the expectation that education would generate the necessary confidence among the tribal people, for interacting with non-tribal people. During 1990-91 and 1991-92, Annual Plans were implemented, separately every year.

Eighth Five-Year Plan:1992-1997

Tribal Sub-Plan strategy with thrust on Modified Area Development Approach continued. Efforts were made to implement development programmes in every remotest part of the country, in order to bring about an overall socio-economic growth of the tribal communities. The main thrust during this Plan was upon income generation programmes with special reference to the primitive tribal communities.

Ninth Five-Year Plan: 1997-2002

Tribal Sub-Plan strategy with thrust on Modified Area Development Approach continued. This plan aimed at the empowerment of the tribal groups. A separate plan of action through micro-projects was formulated for the primitive tribal communities. [During the Ninth Five Year Plan, 75 communities were identified as primitive tribes, in 15 States and Union Territories].

Tenth Five-Year Plan: 2002-2007

Tribal Sub-Plan Strategy with thrust on Modified Area Development Approach continued. The separate plan of action for the primitive tribal communities continued during this Plan.

Eleventh Five-Year Plan: 2007-2012

Tribal Sub-Plan strategy with thrust on Modified Area Development Approach continued. The Primitive Tribal Communities were designated as *'Particularly Vulnerable Tribal Communities'*, at the beginning of the Plan. Special programmes were implemented for their development.

Twelfth Five-Year Plan: 2012-2017

Tribal Sub-Plan strategy with thrust on Modified Area Development

Approach continued along with the special programmes for the development of the Particularly Vulnerable Tribal Communities.

Tribal Development: Present Situation

The Tribal Sub-Plan strategy, which evolved during the Fifth Five-Year Plan, has successfully continued throughout all successive plans since then. the Tribal Sub-Plan has proved to be an important approach for solving the problems of tribal communities. It is noteworthy that a steady development of the tribal communities has been observed since the implementation of the Fifth Five-Year Plan.

Summary and Conclusion

The above review indicates that in the pre-British period there was no policy for the tribal communities. During the British period, even if the British Government kept the tribal communities in isolation, the decisions taken by the British Government largely affected the life of the tribal communities in an adverse manner because the land and forests, the basic livelihood resources of the tribal communities, were snatched by the British Government. Following independence, the Government of India has taken numerous measures to help the tribal communities, including necessary Constitutional and Legal Safeguards for the tribal communities, viz.,

- To protect their own culture and get integrated in the main stream;
- To restore their rights in land and forests;
- To be equal with other citizens;
- Not to be exploited;
- To protect their human rights;
- To get educated and employed; and
- To develop and improve their quality of life.

The strategies for planned development of tribal communities are gaining appreciable momentum since the Fifth Five-Year Plan through the Tribal Sub-Plan Approach/Integrated Tribal Development Programme/Area Development Programme/Problem Solving Approach. These various terms explain the multiple dimensions of the programmes implemented. The results indicate that this strategy is helping to meet the complex challenge of tribal development.

Notes

1. In the ancient land system in India, the *zamindars* were officials under the Kings. the Kings collected a share of the peasants' produce, as protectors of the people, and not as owners of the land. It was the responsibility of the *zamindars* to ensure that the peasants properly paid the land revenue to the Kings.
2. According to *'zamindari'* system introduced by the British Government under the Land Tenure System Act, 1793, the *zamindars* were declared as the proprietors of land, with the right of their ownership being subjected to the regular payment of the land revenue to the Government. With this provision, the *zamindars* acquired the power to make the land as their private property as well as commodity in the market. The system though recognized the rights of the cultivators *(Ryots),* the rights were not clearly defined. This resulted in a situation where the cultivators helplessly suffered oppression and exploitation by the newly created class of *zamindars*. Like the peasants, the tribal communities also suffered beyond imagination. As an outcome of "the Land Tenure System Act, 1793," the land got divided into smaller fractions under the ownership of the feudal lords *(zamindars)*. These *zamindars* represented a class of people, identified as a group *'loyal'* to the foreign British rulers.
3. In response to the agrarian discontent, the British Government introduced the Rent Act, 1859, which was the first tenant law. However, this Act was not useful in addressing the sufferings of the poor peasants. With sympathy for the peasants, the British Government attempted to introduce agrarian reforms. However, all such attempts were not successful because the Legislative Assemblies were dominated by the *zamindars*. The accumulated grievances of the peasants resulted in a movement in 1930s. Tribal movements were launched in conjunction with the peasant movements in 1930s.

References

Bhanage, N.P. (1993), *Tribal Commissions and Committees in India*, Bombay : Himalaya Publications.

Bose, N.K. (1953), *Cultural Anthropology and other Essays*, Calcutta : Indian Associated Publishing Co.

Government of India, New Delhi (1952), *Act for De-notification of the Criminal Tribes.*

Government of India, New Delhi (1976), *Act for Improvement of Economic*

Conditions of Tribal Communities.

Government of India, New Delhi (1976), *Act for Restoration of Agricultural Land, Alienated from Tribal Communities.*

Government of India, New Delhi (1992), *Act on 'Panchayat-Raj' Extension to Scheduled Areas.*

Government of India, New Delhi (2006), *Recognition of Forest Rights of Scheduled Tribes Act.*

Government of India, Parliamentary Committee, New Delhi (1950), Constitution of India.

Government of Maharashtra, Mumbai (2016), *Tribal Sub Plan: Performance Budget.* Ministry of Tribal Development.

Mathur, Hari Mohan (1977), A New Deal for Tribal India in *Anthropology in the Development* New Delhi : Vikas Publishing House Pvt. Ltd., pp. 489-90.

Nehru, Jawaharlal. *A Speech on Return from a Tour of NEFA* (1952).

Nehru, Jawaharlal. *Inaugural Address at the Conference for Tribes and Tribal (Scheduled) Areas*, held at Jagdalpur, 1955.

Nehru, Jawaharlal. Inaugural Speech at the Conference for Tribes and Tribal (Scheduled) Areas, held at New Delhi, 1952, in *'Vanya Jaati'*, Vol. 12, July 1964, No. 3. New Delhi.

Report, *'Bharatiya Adimjati Sevak Sangh'*, New Delhi.

Verma, C., (1990), *Indian Tribes through Ages*, New Delhi : Ministry of Information and Publications, Government of India.

Verrier, Elwin (1963), *A New Deal for Tribal India*, New Delhi : Government of India, Ministry of Home Affairs.

Verrier, Elwin. 'Foreword' to *Philosophy for NEFA*, [First Edition], Shillong (1957): NEFA.

Verrier, Elwin (1959), 'Foreword' to *Philosophy for NEFA*, [Second Edition], Shillong: NEFA.

Vidyarthi, L.P. (Ed.) (1968) Nehru's Approach to Tribal Problems, in *Applied Anthropology in India*, Kitab Mahal, Allahabad.

Vidyarthi, L.P. (Ed.) (1986), *Tribal Development and Its Administration*, New Delhi : Concept Publishing Company.

8

Challenges to the Implementation of Good Governance

A Critique from the Adivasi Perspective

Nirmal Dhanasamy

Introduction

Following the announcement of the 2014 General Elections to the Lok Sabha, the Bharatiya Janata Party (BJP) projected Narendra Modi as the Prime Minister and development and curbing of corruption as its main objectives, leading to the birth of the phrase 'Good Governance.' However, there were apprehensions that behind this take there were hidden notions like neo-liberal ideas "centralisation of power and authoritarian tendencies" (Editorial, *EPW,* 2014:7). This led the corporate world to endorse the candidate because of the promise of a business friendly government. (*ibid.*) Thus, 2014 election became the "biggest corporate heist in history" (*ibid.*), which made things happen by helping BJP spend Rs. 5000 crore just on advertisements (*ibid.*) The Modi campaign was organised around the message of "development" and aimed at taking full advantage of voters' fatigue with the UPA government and anger against rampant corruption during its tenure.

Before Modi's Government came into existence, neo-liberal ideas with globalization had emerged in the Indian continent by the 1990s and Indian economy grew up with neo-liberalism. These twenty seven years (1990-2017) saw many developments especially in the industry, information technology, infrastructures, corporate-run education and health institutes etc. In this growth cantred decade, the amount of production and exports gave a fillip to expectations like better health conditions, economic growth, reduced poverty and better standard of living to all.

However, the amount of growth that had taken place had only led to more alienation of land, migration, unemployment, sickness and inequalities. The number of people who migrated for various reasons, the number of people who were displaced from their lands because of industrialization and the amount of health hazards given in the statistical studies, show that there was an increase in more unhealthy development than good development. The industrial zones that were developed in the last two decades were located mostly in the Adivasi inhabited areas. Consequently, the Adivasi only lost than gaining anything. They have, "lost their livelihood, their skills and knowledge, along with access to resources such as land, hills, forests, rivers" (Mudunuri, 2012:73). To such an extent that they even lost "their Gods" (Padel, 2015:335) and personal lives. Such inhuman results of industrialization and neo-liberal ideologies have only produced, "surplus people who are displaced. These displaced/ marginalised surplus people knowing that there is no hope of survival, have been agitating against these development projects throughout the country" (Mudunuri, 2012:73).

The non-tribal people rarely understand the psyche of the Adivasis. Cultural genocide and human killing has become the invaders' total lack of respect for the Adivasi people's traditions and their connection with their land. The only focus of the newcomer is profit that they can generate from the Adivasi land (Padel, 2015:334). It is in such a situation that the new government has been preaching and propagating neo-liberal ideas in the name of Good Governance.

This chapter will be a critic to the idea of Good Governance from the Adivasi perspective. It will give an idea as to how the implementation of policies and ideas of the government in the Adivasi areas had been a failure in the past two decades, and how it is a challenge for the present government to bring about benefits to the Adivasi communities with the slogan of 'Good Governance'.

What is Good Governance?

In a democratic government, the rulers are elected by the people and entrusted with certain responsibilities and are required to discharge such responsibilities with selfless service. The pursuit of Good

Governance requires greater interaction among the public, the state, private sector and the civil society. Bringing about a right balance for a people-centred development calls for participatory action, transparency, responsibility of individuals, equity, equality, consensus, and accountability. This calls for a responsible contribution from everyone; right from the Prime Minister to the last member of the administration to help the country move ahead towards development. They have to shun greed, arrogance and exploitive nature against the people. It is from this point of view that one has to look at the actions and plans that have been implemented by the governments to know whether Good Governance has arrived in our country.

Is Good Governance Happening?

After three years of BJP government, facts reveal that Good Governance is yet to be experienced in India, especially when it comes to the minorities and the Adivasis in particular. The government has come up with a number of slogans like 'Make in India', '*Sab Ka Saath Sab Ka Vikas*', '*Swatch Bharat Abhiyan*' etc. But, the stream that flows below these slogans makes us wonder whether the call for and assurance of 'Good Governance' is just a dream.

Prime Minister Narendra Modi, who is an efficient orator, is able to captivate his audience with his speeches, in which he does not feel shy to make his neo-liberal ideas known, although such ideas are couched in the name of development. He also brings in the idea of free market and privatisation of economy. But, in a free-market economy, private businessmen control everything. Neo-liberalism, globalisation and global corporations controlling the economy, calls for international trade and investment, where the poor becomes ignored. A flourishing free market ignores workers' rights. A free market economy sans democratic ideals becomes free only for a few. Thus, the slogan '*Sab Ka Saath Sab Ka Vikas*' would sound empty unless the government imposes restrictions keeping in view the lives of the poorer sections. In this situation, we propose to consider in what way good governance has benefited the Adivasi communities and the challenges that the government will have to face in implementation of the policy.

Adivasi Governing System

Adivasi governing system has always been communitarian and non-authoritarian. The saying "good of one is the good of all" had been practiced by them in all its true sense. Thus, their governance system looks for the benefit of all and is community centred. In this homogenous 'oneness of all', the idea of governance was always democratic and the economy had always an inter-tribal connection.

Politically, every tribal group had its own Panchayats, with an elected head and a council which exercised social control of its people. All disputes and offences were brought before the Panchayat. The *'Parha'* system tried to settle inter-village disputes. The decision carried out by the '*Parha*' head was considered with great regard. "The Panchayats were responsible for economic security, maintenance of peace and order, for settling civil and criminal cases, for good relationship with the other clans, neighbours and with the God" (Dhan, 1967:108). This also shows how the tribal members tried to control themselves through their own political organisation. In such a stabilized system of life, the entry of outsiders with their own agenda upset the equilibrium.

Though their education system was very ancient and crude, the youth dormitory system was, "genuine and unadulterated product of their culture" (Roy, 1984:125). Its objectives were to give an economic, social and religious knowledge to the members of their community. It was a place where the young men and women lived together under watchful eyes, learning things for their lives. It was here that they learnt what was freedom and responsibility. In such community living, they learnt their cultural traits, dance, music and singing, and how to go about in life and be a member of the community. They also learnt to observe and participate in the events of their lives, besides their history and traditions. Dhan (1967:96) explains that "instructions were given by the older members of the *dhumkuria,* in folklore, tradition, magical belief and practices, moral code, sexual instruction, dancing and communal activities. Through these they aimed to create group solidarity, self-discipline, obedience and respect to the elders and readiness for mutual help. The indigenous system was designed to train a child for group life and consequently attention was focused on the group rather than the individual. An individual was expected to become exactly like the rest, and he must conform to the customary rules."

Socially their basic organisation was a "domestic group" (Srivatsava, 1992:100). This domestic group or the household possessed a patch of land in which all the children and parents worked together for growing food to meet their needs. In this process, "what was important was to note that they were dependent on the fathers in all respects" (*ibid.*, 101). Ethnographic studies by S.C. Roy, Hoffman, Sachchidananda, L.P. Vidyarthi, K.S. Singh and others tell us that the Adivasis generally followed a joint family system, cultivating a piece of land together, sharing the fruits of their labour with all and lived their life as a family with their traditional and religious belief systems. Thus, for a group of people with an attitude of oneness and their own cultures and traditions, the idea of neo-liberalism and capitalism that accompanies 'Good Governances' has no meaning.

Challenges to Implementation of Good Governance in the Adivasi Areas

The entry of the *Diku* (the outsider) and their ways of dealing with the tribal has brought about tremendous change in the lives of the Adivasis. The *Diku,* being a dominant character or group, has always tried to impose what they thought was right and good for the Adivasis. They insisted that their ways of dealing with the world was the right way and the Adivasi way of interacting with the world was something not acceptable. The imposition of their ideas on the native political systems, educational policies, social traits, cultural trends and economic attitudes in the minds and lives of the Adivasis brought about a lot of psychological, sociological and cultural disadvantages among the Adivasis. Today many Adivasis are unaware of their own cultural, religious, educational, political and social organisms, because of the influence of the outsider.

The *Dikus* look down upon the Adivasis as 'second class citizens'; "primitive, uncivilized, barbaric, uneducated, economically backward, criminal and immoral". They take upon themselves the job of enlightening the Adivasi population according to their own ways. In this process, they overpower and exploit them and cause damage to their lives and culture. Instead of understanding the Adivasis and their way of life, they insist and even force the Adivasis to discard their ways of living, and compel them to learn new things which they consider would bring about development in their lives. Padel (2015:289) says: "Each tribal area has its own local complexities and political subtleties; yet it is clear that what has been imposed on Adivasis in different areas is essentially the same pattern, the same techniques of control imposed through the same colonial rules. It seems that what Europeans imposed on Indians as a whole, certain classes of Indians continue to impose on Adivasis today."

The concept of Good Governance and its implementation in the above scenario seems to be a great challenge. for example, Good governance facilitates corporate houses to take over lands with mineral deposits to produce materials needed for the country's development. The Multinational companies grab the Adivasi lands by luring them with compensation for the land and job for one person of the household. Being simple beings, the Adivasis are easily lured with money and modern ways of living. But, a tribal who sees for the first time a lot of money, lavishly spends it and becomes bankrupt before long. Land being the only source of livelihood for an Adivasi, once the land is taken away from him, he loses everything and becomes a pauper and cannot adjust to a life in the relocated areas. With no other skills, a displaced Adivasi becomes fish out of water. The Adivasis need to be protected from being robbed of their lands through legislation. to cite an example, the Chotanagpur Tenancy Act, 1908, and the Santhal Paragana Tenancy Act, 1949 protected the Adivasis. These Acts said that the Adivasi land cannot be sold to a non-Adivasi at any cost for any purpose. But, on November 23, 2016 the Jharkhand Chief Minister Raghuvar Das (an OBC), got a nod from the legislature which paved the way for industrialisation and implementation of welfare projects by taking up the land of the tribals. Feeling shackled by the said Acts, Raghuvar Das said that "the law restricts the government's say in land acquisition, which is considered a hindrance in initiating development projects for the larger interest of the state." He accused the Christian Missionaries and the Church working in the tribal areas for misguiding the people. the tragedy is that some of the MLAs in the government belonging to the Adivasi communities supported the idea that the outsiders will bring development.

But history tells us that there is little development in Adivasi areas when they are ruled by outsiders. In the 300 to 400 years of tribal history that we know through literature, a mere 5 to 10 per cent Adivasis have benefited and the rest 90 to 95 per cent continue to lead poor lives and live in miserable conditions. For centuries the *Diku* came in only to exploit the Adivasis. People who helped them from such exploitation were criticised, warned, and labelled as foreigners.

It is true that education helps an individual to progress in life. Education had been a way in which the Adivasis were helped to get out of their exploited conditions. Many of the tribal members have been educated and some of them are employed in good posts in the government and private sector. But, "the test of any public aspect of public policy lies in (a) the harmonisation and integration of its diverse components, and (b) its implementation" (Rao, 1999:7). Why there is an increasing gap between the policies of the government and its implementation is what we need to look into. the educational policies that were enacted by the government had western connotation of motivation, which hinges on individualistic and materialistic factor. But the Adivasi connotation to education is traditional, which calls for faith and dedication (Rao, 1999:9). The way in which the educational policies implemented in the Adivasi areas for the Adivasi is more of an imposition with the idea that only a modern education can develop the Adivasis and make the mmodernised. Thus, it became what Foucault calls, "the indignity of speaking on someone else's behalf" (Cited in Marglin, 1990:96).

Under the 'modern' education system, what the Adivasi children study and learn is not their history; but that of others. The medium of instruction is also not theirs. The Adivasi child who uses its own mother tongue in the villages finds it difficult to cope-up with the language of instruction in the schools. Moreover, the attitude of the dominant ethnic groups towards the Adivasi children, their culture, and languages, is an outright rejection of Adivasis, and ridiculing them for using their ways of expressing themselves in their own mother tongue (Midatala, 2000:416). This hurts the Adivasi children leading even to dropouts, semi-literacy, inferiority complex and unwillingness to learn anything new. This brings about exclusive attitude among the Adivasis about oneself. "Several studies in India had documented the huge amount disadvantages faced by children studying through a language that is totally alien to them when they join schools" (Jhingran, 2012:371).

Education should lead a child from "the known to the unknown". The language used in the schools makes the child more confused than being enlightened. For, "the child learns and absorbs the elements of the Adivasi culture through trial and error, play and observation, involving unconscious imitation as well as conscious inculcation" (Jayaram, 2015:27). For teaching the Adivasi children, the government needs to appoint teachers who understand the Adivasi culture better. Such attitude should be a part of good governance. Similarly, socio-cultural practices and habits are part and parcel of every social group.

Eating non-vegetarian food is part of an Adivasis' social habit. But, compelling them to be vegetarian and follow one religion, one culture, and one socio-cultural practice goes against the norms of Good Governance. Overcoming such attitudes is a challenge for the NDA's idea of Good Governance.

Finally, religion is an individual's private sphere. Every individual tries to obtain that spiritual entity called the power (God) in their lives. Though every religion is man-made and practiced by a given group of people, or communities in their own way, nobody must be forced to follow a particular religion. the law holds forcible conversion a crime. But, instances of forcible conversions and reconversions continue in the Adivasi areas, in the name of "one religion one country". If Good Governance were to dawn in this country, the government needs to take action not only on forced conversions but also forced reconversions. Thus, encouraging every community to follow what is precious to them and help them in developing their own lives is another challenge the government has to face.

Conclusion

We feel that in the slogan '*Sab Ka Saath Sab Ka Vikas*', '*Sab Ka*' really means to take care of every aspect of a citizen's life. The Government is required to take care of the culture, art, architecture, educational system, dressing and eating habits, customs, mode of life, language, religious practices etc., of the Adivasis into consideration so that they do not lose their identity. To make governance a good governance, the Government needs to look into every possible need of the people it governs or serves. In this process there shall be no imposition of one's ideas on the other. However, in today's corporate world system, any political party boasting about great changes, has to find acceptable means by which people walk together, work together and progress together, and move ahead. "A government is one that thinks and hears the voices of the poor, must live for the poor, and become only empty phrases, if they do not practice what they say" (Patnaik, 2014:39-40).

So from the Adivasis' point of view, if neo-liberalism were to usher in economic growth, we only see a few jobs created among the Adivasis. Compensating the project affected Adivasis/families and their proper rehabilitation and resettlement is not always done keeping in view their mode of living, lifestyles, sensitivities, their aspirations, and culture etc. Statistics of the displaced Adivasis being employed in the past leaves much to be desired. In the words of Kujur (2008:38), "it can be argued that the government has washed her hands off the responsibility to safeguard the interests of every citizen of the country. The democratic space created at the independence of the nation seems to have shrunk for the vulnerable sections of the society. On the contrary, the democracy of India appears to be the democracy of the rich and the powerful, who understand the language of profiteering and hoarding at the cost of depletion of natural resource and the people living in conformity with them."

What Needs to Be Done?

The Government needs to put Adivasis in the forefront while undertaking developmental activities in tribal areas and consider the real needs of the Adivasi communities. In working out projects for development, it has to work keeping in view the ethos of every society, listen to their aspirations and understand them, so to work for their real benefit. When it comes to the Adivasi community, the government needs to understand their socio-cultural, eco-political, and psycho-spiritual attitudes so as to ensure that benefits of development reach them. It needs to work for the Adivasis with the help of Adivasis. In this context we recall the ideas of Pandit Jawaharlal Nehru, who spoke about how to deal with the Adivasis through his *Panchasheel* and put them into real practice (Cited in Narwani, 2004:14). It reads:

- we should avoid imposing anything on them;
- tribal right in land and forest should be respected;
- train and build up a team of their own people to do the work of administration and development;
- should never over administrate their areas; and
- we should not judge results by statistics of how much money is spend, but by the quality of human character that is evolved.

Then, the government needs to understand the thinking pattern of the Adivasis, so that it can give them a better chance to grow. The government needs to give them the things that they understand and grasp. The government needs to appoint Adivasi men and women to handle the affairs in their own areas. Democracy of an individual community or a race can be only built up by giving them their "autonomy and institutional support" (Mohanty, 2017:66) by self-governance. Thus, we suggest that the government may give the Adivasi community autonomy and self-governance so that they can improve themselves, by ruling themselves. According to Mohanty, 'Adivasi Swaraj' is the only answer for the atrocities that they face everyday in their areas. He quotes from the editorial of *Times of India* dated 26 April, 2017, which says,

> "Approaches to tackling Maoism are inevitably stuck in a security-human rights binary, but this does not have to be the case. In fact the government needs to deploy the right mix of security, development and human rights protection to root out the Maoist problem. This can be done by bringing Adivasi groups, civil society organizations and political parties together, while simultaneously improving intelligence and operational coordination for security forces. It's time to cast aside old shibboleths and adopt a fresh approach."

In dealing with Maoists, the previous government's idea of "clear, hold, develop" could not succeed. The Policy called for a programme "where the armed forces must clear the areas of the Maoists activities through their militaristic operation and that they must establish the authority of the civil administration and only then can they introduce development plans" (Mohanty, 2017:68). Such a policy meant that the outsiders were trying to decide how to handle the situation. But, when there is no co-operation from the insider, i.e. Maoists themselves, the policy becomes unworkable and the struggle continues.

Therefore, wider consultation with the members of the Adivasis and their Panchayats by the policy makers alone will pave the way for proper development of the Adivasis and leads to good governance. Mohanty comments that, "the Panchayats should decide what kind of economic development is needed in their area. They can come up with a plan and for full employment by a certain date, full implementation of the RTE up to high school and universal health care among other things. The present top down model be it under the Planning Commission or the NITI Aayog, with the 'Mission 2017' objectives to clear the region for industries, has to be replaced by Adivasi self-development plan" (2017:70).

Thus, it is a big challenge for the government to serve its people according to the needs of the people and not according to the ideas of politicians alone.

References

Banerjee, Sumanta (2014) "The Resistible Rise of Narendra Modi" in *Economic and Political Weekly*, May 3, Vol. XLIX, No. 18, pp. 10-13.

Dhan, R.O. (1967). *These are my Tribes Men: the Oraons9.*, Ranchi : GEL Church Press.

Editorial, "Anger, Aspiration, Apprehension" in *Economic and Political Weekly*, May 24, 2014, Vol. XLIX. No, 21, pp. 7-8.

Jayaram, N. (2015) *Sociology of Education in India*, Jaipur : Rawat Publications.

Jhingran, Dhir (2012) "Language and Marginalization in Primary Education in India," in Sleeter Christine *et al.* (Eds.), *School Education, Pluralism and Marginality: Comparative Perspectives*, New Delhi : Orient Black Swan, pp. 371-391.

Kujur, Marianus (2008), "Development Induced Displacement in Chhattisgarh: A Case Study from a Tribal Perspective" New Delhi, *Social Action*, A Quarterly Review of Social Trends, January-March, Vol. 58, No. 1. pp. 31-39.

Marglin, Apffel Frederique and Stephen Marglin (Eds.) (1990) *Dominating Knowledge*, London, Oxford : Clarendon Press.

Mohanty, Manoranjan (2017), "Adivasi Swaraj is the Answer to Violence" in *Economic and Political Weekly*, May 27, Vol. LII, No. 21, pp. 66-70.

Mudunuri, Bharathi (2012), "Tribal Women's Perspective on the Land Acquisition Bill" in *Economic and Political Weekly*, May 19, Vol. XLVII, No. 20, pp. 73-77.

Narwani, G.S. (2004) *Tribal Law in India*, New Delhi : Rawat Publications.

Padel, Felix (2015), *Sacrificing People: Invasions of Tribal Landscape*, New Delhi : Orient Black Swan.

Patnaik, Prabhat (2014), "Neo-Liberalism and Democracy" in *Economic and Political Weekly*, April, 12. Vol. XLIX, No. 14, pp. 39-40.

Rani, Midatala. (2000), "Tribal Languages and Tribal Education", in *Social Action*, A Quarterly Review of Social Trends, October-December, Vol. 50. No, 4, pp. 414-419.

Rao, G.R.S. (1999-2000), "Value Premises in the Education System: Gaps between Policy and Implementation", in *Religion and Society*, December, 1999 - March, 2000. Vol. 46, No. 4 and Vol. 47. No. 1. Bangalore : CISRS Publications Trust.

Roy, Sarat Chandra (1984) *The Oraons of Chotanagpur: Their History, Economic Life and Social Organisation*, Calcutta the Brahmo Mission Press.

Srivatsava, A.R.N. (1992), *Changing Values and Tribal Societies*, New Delhi : Inter-India Publication.

Times of India (2017a): "Sukma Attack: Beeûng up Security and Addressing Tribal Grievances Must Go together," 26 April, http://blogs.timesoûndia.

indiatimes.com.

Times of India (2017b): "Will Finalise New Strategy at Meet," 26 April, *Times of India*, http://epaperbeta.timesoûndia.com.

Tirkey, Livinus (1998), *Tribals: Their Languages and Literature,* Ranchi : Don: Bosco Publishers.

Toppo, Sita (1979), *Dynamics of Educational Development in Tribal India*, New Delhi : Classical Publications. (Available at www.corpwatch.org. (Accessed on 28/3/2017). Also, www.outlookindia.com, Vol. LVII. No. 17. p. 11. (Accessed on 24/4/2017), and www.*Times of India*, (Indiantimes.com). November 24, 2016, Ranchi edition. (Accessed on 20/4/2017).

9

Empowering Dalits through Vocational Education

An NGO Discourse and Innovation in Rural Gujarat

R.R. Patil

Introduction

According to the Human Development Report, "deprivation encompasses deprivation in years of life, health, housing, knowledge, participation, personal security and environment". When these different kinds of deprivations interact, they severely constrain human choices" (UNDP: 1997, 25). India is one of the developing countries of the world suffering from human deprivation. The latest HDI available is for 2015, which ranks India at 131. (Reference: Human Development Report 2016. (Available at http://hdr.undp.org/sites/default/files/2016 human development report.pdf) Similarly, of the 90 nations with a high concentration of human deprivation (Human Poverty Index), India ranks as high as 55. Even after seventy years of Independence, the adult literacy rate in India is 74.04 per cent; 23.6 per cent of the population lives below poverty line; sex ratio is (per 1000 male) is 945: infant mortality rate (per 1000 live birth) is 40.5 and 15.2 per cent of the total population are undernourished. Thus, India's progress in Human Development Index is not only slow but varies among different social groups.

The status of the Dalits (Scheduled Castes) is lower in the Human Development Index and they are also the worst sufferers of the practice of untouchability and caste-based discrimination. "If discrimination against women, linguistic communities and Adivasis is based on one or another dimension, discrimination against Dalits is multi-dimensional — economic, social, political, and cultural. Domination over them is cumulative. The most visible sites of domination and discrimination against them are found in Bharat or rural India" (Oommen, 2004:156). They are at the bottom of Human Development Index. Their lives, which have been conditioned by the highest incidence of poverty, illiteracy, ill health, unemployment, powerlessness and various other forms of human deprivation, have pushed them to the edge of the social margin (Singha Roy, 2001:84-86). The Dalits represent only 16.06 per cent of the total population of India as per 2011 Census, but they have the highest level of deprivation compared to the higher caste population. In 2011-12, about 33.8 per cent of rural Dalits and 21.8 per cent of the urban Dalits lived below poverty line (BPL). At 61.4 per cent, employment as casual labour was highest among the Dalits without any job security. The literacy rate among dalit is low as 47 per cent in rural areas and 66 per cent in urban areas. the low literacy rate further affects their representation in higher education and secondary and tertiary sectors of employment. Similarly, it is also found that a vast majority of the Dalits are deprived of access to basic essentials of life, especially safe drinking water, food, housing, minimum clothing, medical care, secured livelihood etc. (NSSO, 2001; Thorat, 2004).

The deprivation of Dalits is also continuing in urban areas. A total 18.7 per cent of the dalit population live in urban India but a majority of them are employed in the unorganised sector, surviving on meagre incomes. According to Harsh Mander, "Eighty-Four per cent of urban SCs work as unskilled labour in the unorganised service sector, e.g. as loaders, brick-kiln, quarry workers etc." (Mander, 2000: 148). Some of the Scheduled Caste communities like the *Bhangi* still perform their traditional occupation of sweeping and scavenging in the cities. By and large, Dalits are highly represented as sweepers and sanitary workers in Class IV position of government services (Chaplin, 2002). The overview of Dalit situation in India shows the prevalence of their multi-dimensional discrimination and marginalisation of Dalits in the society. It also shows that even after seventy years of Independence the caste-system and caste-based discrimination are practiced against the Dalits and a majority of the Dalits are the victims of caste-based discrimination. It is the responsibility of the state, civil society organisation and conscious-sympathetic citizens of India to protect and prevent Dalits from all forms of discrimination and exploitation.

In fact, after Independence, the free Indian state abided by the Socialist-Secular-Democratic values and intervened in favour of the poor in general and Scheduled Castes (SC) and Scheduled Tribes (ST) in particular, through a variety of ways such as reservation of seats in educational institution, employment, and politics. The Constitution of India incorporates several provisions for the removal of untouchability and discrimination against Dalits. There is a Special Component Plan (SCP) in the form of separate budgetary mechanism for the socio-economic development of Dalits. Similarly, the state has given special preferences to Dalits in Health, Education, Rural Development, Slum Improvement and Anti-Poverty Programmes. But, despite these provisions, studies have shown that these measures have only succeeded to a limited extent and most often they have failed to protect the human rights of Dalits (Galanter, 1991; Nandu Ram, 1988; Krishnan, 2002; and Shah, 2002).

Similarly, it has also been observed that although the reservation policy has created a miniscule of better-off sections among Dalits, a majority of the dalit population does not even qualify to avail reservation facilities due to educational backwardness. Thus, their representation is far behind their prescribed quota. Studies have also shown that the practice of Untouchability and Atrocities is the major reason for Human Rights violation of Dalits in India (Navsarjan, 1997; Shah, 2002).

As already stated, the government has been adopting and implementing legal and policy mechanisms for the protection and promotion of scheduled castes/dalit community but information about the contribution of the larger civil society in the empowerment of dalit community remains unrecognized and uncounted. Thus, it is necessary to ascertain and examine the initiatives of civil society organisations, especially Non-Governmental Organisations (NGOs), towards the empowerment of the Dalits. The literature on NGO sector reveals there has been phenomenal growth of NGOs in Gujarat and in India (*see* Kamta, 2000) as well as in other parts of the world (Kramer, 2000). Most of these organisations claim to be at the service of the oppressed and marginalised communities (Choudhary, 2000; Sheth, 1997; Sheth & Sethi, 1991). The type of services provided by these organisations varies widely. These organisations have played and continue to play an important role in responding to the needs of the poor, marginalised and dalit communities in India (Dabhi, 2005; Patil, 2015). However, there is limited literature available on the contributions of NGOs in addressing economic empowerment through vocational education in India.

Thus, keeping in view the limited literature in this area, this chapter explores and highlights the contribution of Navsarjan Trust, an NGO in Gujarat, in the economic empowerment of Dalits through vocational education in the state of Gujarat. This chapter adopts exploratory-*cum*-descriptive research design. We begin with a detailed profile of the NGO and its programmes for the economic empowerment of Dalits. Purposive sampling technique and triangulation are used to scrutinise the data in detail. The collected data has been analysed qualitatively and presented through descriptive writing to understand the NGOs efforts in the economic empowerment of Dalits in rural Gujarat.

Navsarjan Trust (NT)

Navsarjan Trust, an NGO, has its roots in a very prolonged awareness programmes initiated by Church-based organisations in the early seventies in Gujarat. It was the first ever planned programme of Dalit Emancipation to raise the conscience of the community to fight social and economic exploitation. The educational process has led the community to assert its rights over surplus lands and question the unequal and unjust social relationship. The main founding member of NT, Mr. Martin Mackwan recalls:

> "One traumatic experience in 1986 changed our lives. In Golana (Kheda District), the Government gave 33 acres of agricultural land to a Dalit Co-operative. the Government gave another three acres of land to Dalits (*Vankars*) for housing and this land was illegally used by the *Durbars* (a high caste Rajput community) as threshing ground. This was the main issue of confrontation. We were not working with the *Bhangi* Dalit Community (Scavengers). The *Durbars* succeeded in playing the *Vankars* against *Bhangis*. On the morning of 25 January, 1986, the members of the co-operative were attacked; 4 were murdered and 18 wounded. Their houses were burnt. We were shocked and shaken. We registered a case and fought in the courts. the legal battle took 1½ years. We worked very hard with the witnesses, instilled confidence to simply narrate what they saw and not

> be intimidated by cross-questioning. Finally, Kheda District Sessions Court sentenced 14 people to life imprisonment. The Supreme Court upheld the judgement in the case of 10 of the 14 and the remaining 4 were sentenced to 8 years rigorous imprisonment.
>
> What Navsarjan is today has its roots in this experience. We were pained at the lack of unity among the Dalits. The Durbars were thus able to play one against the other. Violence is systematic and it shows its ugly face when *status quo* is challenged. In normal situations of conformity, fear of violence is palpable beneath the surface. We realised that the politics of traditional dalit leaders only accentuated sub-caste identities and conflict. The only way to counter this is through a broad based organisation and using the laws of the land. I learnt the hard way and realised that unless we are able to build a strong local leadership, and that too from the community which had suffered discrimination, we cannot hope to fight the oppressive caste system and its manifestations. Those who have themselves experienced violence and discrimination have a different degree of sensitivity, commitment and also anger against the injustice they faced. Identifying and working with such local leaders, men and women, is the key and we set up Navsarjan Trust in December 1988 to work for Dalits; the most exploited class of the Indian society. The vision behind NT is, *"to strengthen Dalit Non-Cooperation Movement in Gujarat, with caste discrimination as a promotional programme of human rights."*

The NT operates in about 3100 villages in 43 talukas/blocks of 11 districts of Gujarat. Its work is mainly spread in the Rural, Urban, Dalit and Tribal areas. The selection of geographical area for organisational intervention is based on the presence of a good number of Scheduled Castes and the extent of atrocities and violence committed against them. Similarly, NT also covers women, youth, aged, people below poverty line, students, landless labour among Dalits and Tribal (Scheduled Tribes) population. It claims to serve more than 5 lakh dalit population in its operational areas.

The NT has established systematic and well directed programmes towards dalit empowerment. All the programmes and activities have one common agenda: that of strengthening non-cooperation against caste-based discrimination and practice of untouchability. The NT strongly believes that caste-based discrimination and atrocities against Dalits will disappear by systematic intervention and broad-based movements. The NT has a total of six major programmes, viz. (a) Legal Aid and Legal Education, (b) Dalit Shakti Kendra, (c) Educational Programme, (d) Campaign, Training and Mobilisation (e) Abolition of Manual Scavenging and Rehabilitation of Scavengers, and (f) Women's Empowerment. Out of these, the first four programmes are directed towards the social, economic, educational and political empowerment of dalit.

Dalit Shakti Kendra (DSK)

The DSK is one of the important and major programmes of the NT; earlier named Vocational Training Centres. The Dalit Shakti Kendra meaning ***Dalit Empowerment Centre*** better describes the aim of the programme. It does not only teach a number of vocations for economic independence but also acts as an economic empowerment centre for dalit youth.

The NT strongly believes that caste-based discrimination has penetrated in all the aspects of the society to such an extent that even the modern educational institutions and companies have also become parties to it. Due to discriminations in the modern institutions, Dalits do not have access to modern education and jobs in the market. Majority of the dalit school drop-outs of rural India do not even get entry to any vocational training institutes and remain deprived from technological education and end up as unskilled labour in the unorganised sector. Thus, to access technical education and generate economic independence among the dalit youth, the NT has set up its own vocational training institute in 1999 at Nani Devti in Sanand Taluka of Ahmedabad District. The DSK is run by Dalits for Dalits. The main objectives of DSK are as follows:

(a) To create vocational opportunities and support systems for Dalits whereby their dependence for survival on traditional and caste-based occupations could be reduced/eliminated;
(b) To train dalit youth in vocational-oriented technical training in different disciplines with a view to making them financially self-dependent/independent in life;

(c) To improve their general living standards, develop proper attitudes and make them socially responsible citizens;
(d) To strengthen the spirit of self-confidence, self-respect, values of disciplined life and respect for dignity of labour through hard work, dedication, mutual cooperation and community life; and
(e) To assist the trained youth in finding suitable jobs, in arranging loans for own small independent businesses and in getting admission to educational institutions, defence services, the police and alike.

The establishment of DSK was a policy level decision taken by the Board of Trustees. However, the planning of the programme in terms of the actual number of courses, type of courses, time schedule, infrastructural facilities, intake policy, management, curriculum design, teaching methodology, teachers, rules and regulations are meticulously planned by the founding member of NT along with the senior programme officer, teachers and staff of the DSK. Similarly, the DSK planning is flexible and market-oriented. the plans are made keeping in view the sustenance of the programme as well as fulfilling the need of the market. Many new courses are introduced and old training courses have been abandoned due to the market trends. The demands and intake of students also influenced the planning process of DSK by an increase in specific courses according to the needs. The programme planning process has designed courses in such a way that students will be given 20 per cent classroom instructions and 80 per cent practical training in designated workshops with necessary tools and training materials. The DSK offers short two to three month training courses and at present there are 13 different training courses such as Tailoring, Driving and Servicing, Auto/Motor Mechanic, Police Training, Computer Course, Motor Rewinding, Carpentry, Textile Designing, Fabrication, Micro-concrete Roofing, Wireman, Beauty Parlour, Video and Photography. A total 240 students (majority of Dalits) are undergoing training.

The DSK started with meagre resources and infrastructural facilities. The founding members approached and convinced funding agencies with the idea of setting up a vocational training centre for Dalits. Appreciation of the idea by the funding agencies and their financial aid helped the NT to develop infrastructural facilities, acquire training equipment and meet other recurring expenditure. The fee collected from the students is a regular source of income for meeting the day-to-day expenses of the DSK.

Implementation of the DSK programme relies on the programme coordinator, 14 teachers and the field staff of the NT. The programme implementation starts with the dissemination of information about the training courses by the 150 NT field staff in the operational areas and making the dalit youth aware of the application process. Additionally, information about the training programmes is also spread through 'Dalit Shakti' magazine brought out by the NT. Similarly, the local people participate in the annual cultural programme of the DSK and get oriented about the aims of the DSK. Student participation in all the activities is overwhelming. Adhering to all the rules and regulations of the programme, the students wash their own cloths, make their own beds and clean the campus regularly, besides learning about equality, gender non-discriminations and disciplined life.

The DSK being one of the education-*cum*-employment generation programmes of the NT, the goal of the NT is to teach the students modern technical skills and make them able to start their own small businesses or become self-employed and reduce their dependence on the dominant castes. The NT strongly believes that through the modern technical skills and self-employment, dalit youth can break the traditional division of labour of caste system and free themselves from the caste-based discriminations of the labour market.

Thus, the DSK is one of the NGO programmes in Gujarat implemented by Dalits for Dalits, meeting their educational needs and ensuring their economic empowerment. the DSK efforts are directed towards economic empowerment through self-employment and entrepreneurship among Dalits through technical education. It also addresses the economic empowerment aspects such as access and control over productive resources, ability to participate in productive activities and gain economic independence.

Impact of Dalit Shakti Kendra (DSK) on Dalits

We have so far highlighted the initiatives of Navsarjan Trust through DSK for employment and livelihood generation among the Dalit community in Gujarat. We now propose to describe the impact of DSK on the dalit students in general and on their employment and livelihood opportunities in particular. the aim is to understand whether such a vocational training programme can be a successful model to empower the Dalit community socially and economically. The present study could find two impacts of DSK, viz. Economic Impact and, Socialisation and Personality Development.

Economic Impact

The data related to the economic impact, especially the employability of DSK students has been collected from the programme co-ordinator through informal discussion. According to the programme co-ordinator, the employability of the DSK students has been very satisfactory and a majority of the graduates had a regular job after the training. Students' enrolment in the DSK has been on the increase despite the fact that DSK is NGO-run and relatively new initiative in the given geographical area. the programme co-ordinator states that the unemployment rate among dalit students is gradually coming down and a majority of young Dalits are getting regular jobs. It thus transpires that DSK's systematic and persistent efforts towards economic empowerment of Dalits in Gujarat have resulted in the emergence of a new labour market for the Dalits in Gujarat.

Socialisation and Personality Development

Data relating to socialization pattern and personality development of DSK students shows the impact of DSK training on the awareness of students and family members. The programme co-ordinator reveals that apart from vocational training/education, the DSK is equally concerned about the personality development of students through rigorous daily routine at DSK. It is learnt that DSK has also been imparting 'soft skills' such as confidence building, communication skills, self-awareness and self-respect etc. to build a positive attitude and behaviour among dalit students. Such training makes the students become socially aware, self-disciplined, independent, cooperative and respecting the equality both at home and in the society. The DSK training also had positive impact on the families of the trainees in developing positive ideas, values, attitude, self-respect, dignity and equality.

Conclusion

The emergence of Navsarjan Trust and its DSK programme in Gujarat is a planned effort towards economic and social inclusion of the marginalised dalit community. It is a local Gujarati initiative for the economic as well as social empowerment of Dalits in the midst of deprivation and marginalisation in the society. The DSK's vocational training programmes have created employment opportunities leading to the economic well-being among the graduates of the DSK. The findings clearly show that Navsarjan's DSK has a positive impact on the marginalised groups, especially Dalits, in Gujarat. It has helped to bring down casual and daily wage labour and opening up a new labour market for the dalit community. Apart from positive economic impact, there has been a great impact on the social aspects of the DSK graduates, as the DSK has been able to inculcate in them a positive attitude and beliefs.

Thus, Navsarjan's DSK does not function as a vocational training centre alone but has been aiming to empower the Dalits. At the DSK, the Dalit students not only acquire technical skills needed for gainful employment, but also are grounded with values and attitude required for leading a respectable life in the society. This combination of vocational education along with personality development is a unique approach of DSK for the empowerment of Dalits in Gujarat. In concluding, we strongly suggest the undertaking of a quantitative research to examine the various aspects of DSK on the empowerment of Dalits in Gujarat. Similarly, it is also suggested that a comparative study could also be undertaken to understand the role and impact of Governmental and Non-Government vocational educational institutes in the economic empowerment of Dalits in India.

References

Baviskar, B.S. (2001), NGOs and Civil Society in India, in *Sociological Bulletin*, 50(1).

Chaplin, S.E. (2002), Scavengers Still Marginalized, in Ghanshyam Shah (Ed.) *Dalits and the State*, New Delhi : Concept Publishing Company.

Choudhary, A.K. (2002), NGOs and their Role in Poverty Alleviation. In Kanta Prasad (Ed.) *NGOs and Socio-Economic Development Opportunities*, New Delhi : Deep & Deep Publication.

Dabhi, J. (2002), Development and Social Transformation: Role of the Voluntary Sector, in *Social Change*, 34(1).

Dabhi, J. (2005), NGOs Response to Violence against the Marginalised and Discriminated Communities, in *Social Action*, 55(1).

Dhanagare, D.N. (1988), Action Group and Social Transformation in India, in *Lokayan Bulletin*, VI (5).

Galanter, M. (1991), *Competing Equalities: Law and the Backward Classes in India,* Delhi : Oxford University Press.

Garain, S. (1994), Government-NGO Interface in India: An Overview, in *the Indian Journal of Social Work*, LV (3).

Gil, D.G. (1998), *Confronting Injustice and Oppression: Concepts and Strategies for Social Workers*, New York : Columbia University Press.

Government of India, National Sample Survey Organization, *Employment and Unemployment Situation among Social Groups in India 1999-2000*, 55(469), MSPI, New Delhi (2001).

Hirway, I. (1995), Selective Development and Widening Disparities in Gujarat, in *Economic and Political Weekly*, 30(41-42).

Iyengar, S. (1998), Voluntary Initiatives for Tribal Development in Gujarat, in *Journal of Entrepreneurship*, 7(2).

Jain, R.B. (1997), NGOs in India: Their Role, Influence and Problems. In Noorjahan Bava (Ed.) *Non-Governmental Organizations in Development: Theory and Practice,* New Delhi : Kanishka Publishers.

Jain, R.B. (Ed.) (1994), *NGOs in Development Perspective*, Delhi : Vivek Prakashan.

Kamta, P. (Ed.) (2000), *NGOs and Socio-Economic Development Opportunities,* New Delhi : Deep & Deep Publications.

Kothari, R. (1984), The Non-Party Political Process, in *Economic and Political Weekly*, XIX (5).

Kramer, R.M. (2000), "A Third Sector in the Third Millennium", *Voluntas*, II (1).

Krishnan, P.S. (2000), Untouchability and Atrocities, in Ghanshyam Shah (Ed.) *Dalits and the State*, New Delhi : Concept Publishing Company.

Kropac, M. (2007), Dalit Empowerment and Vocational Education: An Impact Study, *Working Paper Series,* Volume II, Number 03, Indian Institute of Dalit Studies, New Delhi.

Mander, H. (2002), Status of Dalits and Agenda for State Intervention, in Krishnan, P.S. (2000), *op. cit.*, Government of India, National Commission for Scheduled Castes and Scheduled Tribes, (2001) *Sixth Report, 1999-2000 and 2000-01,* New Delhi.

Navsarjan, Trust, *Gujarat Dalit: Garib Hak Rakshak Samiti*, Navsarjan Trust: Ahemdabad (1997).

Oommen, T.K. (2001), Multiple Modernities and the Rise of New Social Movements: the Case of India in *Indian Social Science Review*, III (I).

Oommen, T.K. (2004) Nation, Civil Society and Social Movements, in *Essays in Political Sociology,* New Delhi : Sage Publications.

Pandey, S.R. (1991) *Community Action for Social Justice: Grassroots Organizations in India*, New Delhi : Sage Publications.

Patil, R.R. (2005), *Empowering Dalits: Non-Governmental Organizations in Western India,* New Delhi : Manak Publications Private Limited.

Patnaik, B.K. and Panda, B. (2005), Perceiving the Role of Grassroots NGOs: From the New Social Movement Perspective, in *Social Change*, 35(3).

Pawar, S.N., *et al.* (Eds.) (2004), *NGOs and Development: The Indian Scenario*, New Delhi : Rawat Publications.

Rajasekhar, D. (2000), Non-Governmental Organizations (NGOs) in India: Opportunities and Challenges, in *Journal of Rural Development*, 19(20).

Ram, Nandu (1998) The *Mobile Scheduled Castes: Rise of a New Middle Class,* Delhi : Hindustan Publishing Corporation.

Sarkar, A.K. (2005), *NGOs: The New Lexicon of Health Care*, New Delhi: Concept Publishing Company.

Sarkar, P. and Mukherjee, D. (2000) NGOs and India's Health Sector, In Kamta Prasad (Ed.) *NGOs and Socio-Economic Development Opportunities*, New Delhi : Deep & Deep Publications.

Shah, G. (2002) *Dalits and the State*, New Delhi : Concept Publishing Company.

Sheth, D.L. and Sethi, H., The NGO Sector in India: Historical Context and Current Discourse', *Voluntas*, 2(2).

Singha Roy, D.K. (Ed.) (2001) *Social Development and the Empowerment of Marginalized Groups: Perspectives and Strategies*, New Delhi : Sage Publications.

Thorat, S. and Mahamallik, M. (2006), "Human Development and the Status of Social Group in Gujarat", *Working Paper Series, I* (06), Indian Institute of Dalit Studies.

UNDP, (1997a), *Human Development Report*, Delhi : Oxford University Press.

UNDP (1997b) *Human Development Report in South Asia*, Delhi : Oxford University Press.

UNDP, (2001) *Human Development Report*, Delhi : Oxford University Press.

World Bank. (1995) *Working with NGOs: A Practical Guide to Operational Collaboration between the World Bank and Non-Governmental Organizations*, World Bank (Operations Policy Department), Washington, DC.

10

Role of Civil Society in Ensuring Good Governance

Ravindra Singh

Introduction

Governance is the process by which a society manages its affairs through the mechanism of the state. The goal of Good Governance is achieved with People's effective participation, consensus building, and inclusiveness, effectiveness with efficiency, responsiveness and accountability. Good Governance is putting people at the centre of the development process. This chapter aims to analyse and assess the role of Civil Society Organisations in ensuring Good Governance. It also highlights the role of CSO in ensuring greater accountability and transparency and explores the contribution made by CSOs in various roles such as being a watchdog, an advocate, an educator, agitator, and service provider etc.

India has a representative parliamentary democracy, entrusting the decision-making to a small group of elected representatives. This could result in "government of the people" becoming a government 'off' the people. Progressive marketisation of traditional government functions has widened this gap. There is a wide gap between the not-so-efficient state and the profit-alone-matters private sector, which calls for a third sector to bridge it. This is how a Civil Society Organisation is seen today.

Civil Society Organizations (CSO)

The term "civil society organisation" refers to "the wide diversity of not-for-profit, non-state organisations as well as community-based associations and groups (as distinct from both the governmental and business sectors) that advance the cause of a collective or public good. These organisations are also referred to as non-profit organisations, Non-Governmental Organisations (NGOs), charities, and voluntary organisations.[1] Civil Society Organisations Act through social capital, i.e. the capacity of people to act together willingly in their common and long term interest. Hence, civil society can be conceptualized as a space where people can pursue self-defined goals in an associational area of common concerns.

Governance

Governance refers to the decision making processes in the administration of an organisation. As per Webster's Third New International Dictionary (1986) it is "the act or process of governing, specifically authoritative direction and control." This elucidation specifically focuses on the efficiency of the executive branch of the government. The British Council uses a broader definition: "Governance involves interaction between the formal institutions and those in the civil society. Governance refers to a process whereby elements in society wield power, authority and influence and enact policies and decisions concerning public life and social upliftment." The World Bank's focus on governance reflects the global thrust toward political and economic liberalisation. Such a governance approach highlights issues of greater state responsiveness and accountability and the impact of these factors on political stability.

Good Governance

The World Bank, for the first time in 1989 has highlighted the concept of good governance. From the World Bank's perspective, 'good governance' means sound public management with the following four dimensions:

- Public sector management;
- Accountability;
- Legal framework for development; and
- Information and transparency.

In 1992, the Bank's document *Governance and Development* said, "Good governance is central to creating and sustaining an environment which fosters strong and equitable development and it is an essential complement to sound economic policies." Taking indication from World Bank guidelines, O.P. Minocha defines the criteria of good governance as "political accountability, availability of freedom, law abiding, bureaucratic accountability, information available transparently, being effective and efficient, and cooperation between government and society."

Certainly good governance refers to civil society as much as it refers to the state—it is as much about democratising the social sphere as it is about democratising the state. The task of counterbalancing the powers of the state means counterbalancing the perpetuation of hegemonies in society (Tandon and Mohanty, 2002). If this perspective is lost, good governance will merely become another project, which enables the market and makes the state more efficient.[2]

The beginning of good governance, the promotion of which the NGOs believe is their task as civil society organisations, legitimises the state which performs well according to the parameters of governance. For instance, one of the ways of promoting transparency is through right to information. But is the right to information sufficient to empower the ordinary people against the might of the state? Does good governance tell us what we should do if the information we receive does not serve the interest of the marginalised people? A stress merely on the right to information will not in itself lead to social action; it may very well make NGOs content that they have achieved their goal by finding some information for the consumption of people. How do we weave an agenda of social action around that piece of information? (Ranjita Mohanty).

Promoting Good Governance

Besides counter-balancing the state, CSO are also expected to make the state accountable through monitoring its activities and making it transparent. They are also expected to promote democracy through free and fair elections, promotion of the rule of law, and protection of human rights. NGOs thus see themselves engaged in tasks like citizens monitoring the budget of the state, promoting transparency through right to information, sensitising citizens through voter-awareness, voter registration drive, and checking corruption by the state institutions etc.

Core Ingredients

Governance is the process by which a society manages itself through the means of the state. The core ingredients of good governance are: People's effective participation, transparency, responsiveness, consensus building, equity and inclusiveness, rule of law, effectiveness and efficiency, accountability, and strategic vision. These are significantly value-laden and constitute the foundations of democracy. Numerous Administrative Reforms Commissions have produced no substantial impact on the quality of governance. the stress now is on facilitating external pressure from citizens on the system to improve through the Right to Information Act, Consumer Protection Act, Citizens Charters, Whistle-blower Protection, e-governance, Report Cards, Democratic Decentralisation, Public Interest Litigation etc.

Governance has three levels: internal systems and procedures; cutting edge systems and procedures; and checks-and-balances. At level (a), the civil society can influence policy and project formulation through membership of committees, submission of memoranda directly or through elected representatives, and interactive rule-making in the implementation of policies, projects and schemes affecting citizens. At level (b) the maximum day-to-day interaction between the government and the citizens takes place and the popular image of governance is formed. At level (c) Interactions of civil society, infrequent but important, will be more of an exposure of irregularities rather than steps for improvement in the quality of governance.

Functional Contribution of Civil Society's to Good Governance

Civil society's functional contribution to good governance could be in the form of:

- Watchdog against violation of human rights and governing deficiencies;
- Advocate of the weaker sections' points of view;
- Agitator on behalf of aggrieved citizens;
- Educating citizens on their rights, entitlements and responsibilities and the government about the pulse of the people;
- Service provider to areas and people not reached by official efforts or as government's agent ; and

- Mobiliser of public opinion for or against a programme or policy.

Civil society acts through 'social capital'— the capacity of people to act together willingly in their common long-term interest. Social capital is strong in a homogeneous, egalitarian society.[3]

The Role of Civil Society in Good Governance

CSO are expected to make the state accountable through monitoring its activities and making it transparent. They are also expected to promote democracy through free and fair elections, promotion of the rule of law and protection of human rights. CSO get engaged in tasks like citizens monitoring the budget of the state, promoting transparency through RTI, voter-awareness, voter's registration drive etc. Civil society as facilitators or driving forces acts as an instrument of a state to ensure good governance and work to bridge the gap between the law and its actual implementation (rule of law). the most important test for civil society is to deal with the complexity of its internal and external problems. Social capital... as the willingness of citizens to trust others including members of their own family, fellow citizens, and people in general (Whiteley, 2003) as trust, norms of reciprocity and networks of civil engagement (Putnam, 1992) Therefore, the principal role of civil society is to produce more social capital by fostering trust, promoting norms of reciprocity and creating more networks of civic engagement. Good governance cannot be achieved in one go. It has to grow organically from the very roots of the civil society. Without good governance, the rule of law, respect for human rights, and democracy, no amount of development assistance will be helpful.

Role of Civil Society Organisations: Case Study

The following section is an attempt to examine and highlight the role and relevance of certain organisations that have been silently but significantly working on issues of good governance.

Bringing Grassroots Democracy to Life: MKSS Campaign in Rajasthan

Panchayat elections in Rajasthan have witnessed a new attempt at transparency and efforts to revitalise grassroots democracy. The Mazdoor Kisan Shakti Sangathan (MKSS) has been working in some districts of central/southern Rajasthan for more than a decade, organising and empowering the poor and marginalised. These attempts have focused on their campaign for the right to information for a cleaner and accountable government. In the Panchayat elections in 2000, out of the three MKSS workers who contested for the post of the Sarpanch, two were successful. By contesting Panchayat elections on the basis of transparency and accountability, the MKSS has made an attempt to lay the foundations for ethical participation in the political process. The MKSS workers and their supporters contested for post of Sarpanch and President of Panchayat Samiti. It was also decided that these candidates would face the electorate with a 'people's manifesto'(the *jan ghoshana patra*); a set of promises that were arrived at collectively, after a year of discussion on various issues relevant to their region. The manifesto contained the following:

- The Sangathan's stand on social issues like child marriages, the custom of *mrityubhoj*, alcoholism, corruption, and employment guarantee act;
- The *jan ghoshana patra* also stated that the MKSS candidates and MKSS-supported candidates will not spend more than Rs. 2,000 on their campaign expenditure. The reason behind the expenditure limit at Rs. 2,000 against the official limit is Rs. 5,000 was to ensure that even the poor could participate in elections. The participation of the poor in local institutions is seen as an essential step towards gaining control over the direction of development;
- Through *Padayatras*, meetings at *chaurahas*, *jan manch* etc., the candidates were forced to discuss the 'people's manifesto' prepared by the Sangathan face to face. This and distributing pamphlets contributed to a healthy and energetic debate on various issues related to grassroots democracy. Much of the campaigning by the candidates was done through *padayatras* with the local candidate and other villagers in haul. The meetings were publicised through door to door canvassing and through announcements at congregation of children. The children were taught some of the slogans and an MKSS worker led them around the village as they urged people to come to the *chaupal* for the meeting.

The meeting began with an introduction to the Sangathan and its work and moved on to discuss the people's manifesto. The issues discussed in the *ghoshana patra* were that of every MKSS (or MKSS-supported) candidate will not be taking or giving bribes as Sarpanch, not spending more than Rs. 2,000 on campaigning etc. The activists explained the link between big expenditure campaigns and corruption. For example, a Sarpanch often faces the problem of getting work sanctioned for their Panchayat. For, obtaining the required sanction invariably involves greasing someone's palms at the Panchayat Samiti level. Often, this money is recovered from villagers by demanding bribes to get their work done. Distribution of alcohol and *gur,* and the use of jeeps are frequently used means of buying votes and contribute to campaign expenditure.

- The entire chain of corruption was explained to the gathered villagers, who were told that low cost elections not only allowed the poor to participate, but also made corruption-free Panchayats a possibility. The more a candidate spends on his campaign, the more money he will want to 'recover' once elected. By voluntarily keeping campaign expenditure within (or below) the official limit, the Sangathan makes clear the absolute necessity of a mandatory limit on expences which is actually complied with. There was a lot of scepticism about the possibility of winning elections (let alone running a Panchayat) on the strength of honesty and transparency. One such cynic was Mohan Singh, an ex-ward member of Kushalpura Panchayat, who said at the Dhorela village meeting that if one followed the rules laid down by the MKSS in their manifesto, there can be no development in the village. However, recounting the experience of two Sangathan activists, Tej Singh (Todgarh) and Narayan (Kushalpura) as Sarpanchs, the MKSS was able to counter such cynicism. Tej Singh spent Rs. 840 on his election campaign and Narayan Singh won in spite of spending only Rs. 1,200. In these two Panchayats, the Sarpanchs claimed complete transparency and honesty. They neither received, nor paid bribes. Being organised and being a part of a collective, they were able to resist pressure 'from above'. Narayan Singh - the erstwhile Sarpanch of Kushalpura, challenged anyone to point out a single instance of misappropriation in the Panchayat in the last five years. He could face the villagers with confidence as the MKSS had just completed social audits in these villages.

- The social audit is a unique process where all the records of the Panchayat are shared with villagers, scrutinised by them and openly verified in every ward of the Panchayat. MKSS members believe that a prudent and transparent election campaign is a necessary condition to ensure such honesty. Spreading rumours is another strategy used by many in the pre-election days. The face-to-face meeting gave Narayan an opportunity to put his point of view across because opponents were spreading rumours about some of his decisions as Sarpanch. It was alleged that Narayan had moved the ration shop to Devdoongri (his own village). However, Narayan explained that the distribution of grain from Devdoongri was a temporary measure and the result of a government order. Similarly, the residents of Dhorela were upset that their village had no Anganwadi centre. Once again, Narayan clarified that this was due to: (1) government norms for opening Anganwadi centres, first in habitations that have a population of more than 500 and then in smaller habitations; and (2) the fact that Dhorela had been carved out as a revenue village only after 2000, and its recognition as a separate village in government records had a direct bearing on the decision to open an Anganwadi centre there.

The high interest shown in Panchayat elections indicates that Panchayati Raj Institutions (PRIs) can be a very important link in strengthening Indian democracy.

Challenges Ahead

The meetings and the MKSS' experience in running Panchayats over the past five years highlighted some of the limitations of the Panchayati Raj system. As questions raised at the Dhorela meeting demonstrated, the Sarpanchs have little control over most important decisions pertaining to their Panchayats. They are held accountable for such decisions, but there is no legitimate channel for them to influence such decisions. This is all the more a pity as direct interaction with elected representatives of PRIs is possible in a way that it is not in the case of MLAs and MPs.

Direct interaction was feasible not only because of a smaller-electorate to representative ratio, but also because of the absence of social distance as in the case of MPs and MLAs. Rather, the system seems designed to undermine people's participation in decision-making and to furthering corrupt practices. Yet another instance of this is that Sarpanchs are paid only Rs. 400 per month (compared with Rs. 25,000 per month for MLAs). Given the running around that a Sarpanch is expected to do in the course of his job and the full-time nature of his work, the poor salary of a Sarpanch promotes corruption. Narayan and Tej Singh were, therefore, supported by the MKSS during their term as Sarpanchs with their salaries set at minimum wage level.

The Sangathan workers organise vigilance committees consisting of about 15 people each, with the responsibility of keeping a constant vigil on whoever is elected, and in ensuring that all decisions that are taken are in accordance with the people's demands. Panchayat elections are notorious for the 'decentralisation' of corruption. The MKSS campaign has demonstrated that these elections provide an opportunity to 'democratise' ethics and commitment as a basis for political participation.[4]

Some Strategies for Ensuring Efficient Governance Amid Global Efforts to Operationalise the Concept of Good Governance

Kerala has shown that a people-oriented, multi-sectoral approach to health and a commitment to equitable and universal access to basic social services contribute to equitable human development. The case of Kerala also shows that such an equity based approach can even be pursued with modest economic growth. This experience contradicts conventional wisdom that high economic growth is a prerequisite for sound social development. Muhammad Yunus, founder of the Gramin Bank of Bangladesh and internationally known for extending microcredit to the poor often tells development experts: "Poverty is not created by poor people. It is produced by our failures to create institutions to support human capabilities."

An excellent example of the fruits of cooperation between the State and individuals can be seen in the case of Ralegaon Siddhi in Maharashtra. The Ralegaon Siddhi Project covered four watersheds and a total geographical area of about 892 hectares. The State's involvement ended after the budgeted expenditure was reached. However, the project was completed by the people by borrowing from banks and through contribution from the villagers. The success of the conversion of this poverty stricken village into a self-sufficient one is to be credited to the leadership of Anna Hazare, who led the villagers into developing a series check-dams, cemented *bandharas* and *nullah* bunds. These measures increased the infiltration of harvested water and recharged ground water acquirers. Farmers can now grow two or three crops every year including fruits and vegetables. Equitable distribution of water is assured through a water supply association. the involvement of all the villagers has made this a sustainable project. Examples like this should be publicized across the country, especially in villages. Villagers elsewhere may feel motivational and encouraged if they know of others who were in a similar state of poverty but who as a result of their own efforts have come out of poverty.[5]

Lok Satta, an NGO based in Hyderabad, is yet another good example of promoting many facets of good governance. It vociferously demanded the passing of the Right to Information Act, to make information currently under the control of public authorities accessible to the public. This in turn would promote openness, transparency and accountability in administration. *Lok Satta* runs a People's Watch Movement, in which the citizens monitor the activities of the state. Issues ranging from police competence, getting passport and birth certificates, delivery at petrol pumps, to bribery at the property registration office, are covered under the People's Watch Movement. *Lok Satta* has trained over ten thousand young people to act as active and assertive citizens. It also runs an Election Watch Campaign, which includes the verification of the criminal background of the candidates contesting elections, verification of the electoral rolls and focusing on key electoral reforms."

Conclusion

Civil Society on its own cannot play its full potential role in enforcing good governance in India except when extraordinary leadership overcomes narrow loyalties, or when an issue is of common, major concern to all sections of the people (like natural calamities). Smaller units of governance and decentralisation of governance are, therefore, indispensable in India.

Efforts to improve the quality of governance will be unsuccessful if the quality and calibre of the political executive is not good enough. Civil society needs to note the deterioration in the quality, integrity and commitment of the elected representatives and the criminalisation of politics. Voter education, electoral reforms and periodical highlighting of the performance (or non-performance) of elected representatives are high priority items in civil society's agenda. Four important roles that civil society should play include:

- Holding government accountable;
- Influencing government policy and lobbying for change;
- Demanding efficient public services; and
- Delivering essential services, where there is an added advantage or greater capacity.

Good governance in CSOs is the exercise of power and authority, based on the established values of the organisation, to achieve the mission and make proper use of resources. Good governance involves providing direction and oversight so that the organisation knows where it is going; monitoring its progress; protecting the interests of the organisation's beneficiaries; and ensuring accountability to society, beneficiaries, and donors through a that is transparent, equitable, and appropriate to the needs of the beneficiaries. The CSO have a significant role to play at all levels so that they can provide a full civil society contribution towards the development and monitoring of strategies and implementation processes. Given the current diversity in approaches and capacities of NGOs, extensive work is required to be done to see that the NGOs can contribute both individually and collectively in the most effective manner to the development of civil society in developing countries. In establishing participative systems for strategy development, monitoring and evaluation, it is essential to provide effective checks and balances so that there is full accountability, not just on the government side, but also on the part of civil society actors.

Notes

1. Available at http://www.thehindu.com/todays-paper/tp-features/tp-openpage/the-role-of-civil-society-in-good-governance/article2276002.ece

2. Mohanty, Ranjita. Civil Society and NGOs, in *the Indian Journal of Political Science*, Vol. 63, No. 2/3 (June-September 2002), pp. 213-232, Indian Political Science Association.
3. Available at https://www.msh.org/sites/msh.org/files/emanager_2009-no2_governance-english_0.pdf
4. Khera, R. (2005). Bringing Grassroots Democracy to Life: MKSS Campaign in Rajasthan. *Economic and Political Weekly*, 40(8): 725-728. (Available at http://www.jstor.org/stable/4416230).
5. Bhatt, M., and Bhatt, Y. (2004). Good Governance: A Promise for Justice, in *The Indian Journal of Political Science*, 65(2): 221-234. (Available at http://www.jstor.org/stable/41855810).

Referencs

Available at http://www.humsec.eu/cms/fileadmin/user_upload/humsec/SAc_07_PPP/ZIVANOVIC_PPP.pdf

http://www.dochas.ie/sites/default/files/Dochas_Governance_ and_Civil_Society.pdf.

Mohan, Sudha. "Role and Relevance of Civil Society Organisations", in *The Indian Journal of Political Science*, Vol. 63, No. 2/3 (June-September 2002): 193-211, Indian Political Science Association. (for example the Resource Alliance.org).

Resource Alliance, "Glossary," (Available at http://www.resource-alliance.org/resources/75.asp)

World Bank. (1992). *Governance and Development*. Washington D.C . The World Bank.

11

Institutions and Weaker Sections

The Dilemma of Inclusion and Exclusion

Prashant Bansode

Introduction

For inclusion of the weaker sections, the institutions of the society, especially the state and the bureaucracy, play a vital role. Especially in the context of ensuring rights, the state is the institution which has not only to guarantee the rights but also ensure, through the bureaucratic machinery, that the rights are availed by the weaker sections.

In India the Scheduled Castes and Scheduled Tribes are the weaker sections. There is a wide disparity in the development between these socio-economic classes and others. The development of weaker sections lags behind the general population in many aspects. Land is one of the important sources, especially in the agriculture dominated country like India. The Scheduled Castes are deprived of this source, as their role in the traditional caste hierarchy and rural economy is to serve the upper castes and work as village servants. The Scheduled Tribes have a different issue. Though geographically and socially isolated, they are exploited, along with their natural resources, by non-tribals, especially the moneylenders, traders and upper castes. The Scheduled Tribes are also driven into the forced labour system in India. Thus, for the liberation of the weaker sections in the rural economy, owning land is important so that they could lead life with dignity and free of exploitation. The data presented in Table 11.1 shows the disparity between the weaker sections and the general population with regard to landholdings.

From the Agricultural Census for 2010-11 (Table 11.1), it is clear that the proportion of Scheduled Caste landholders and the average

Table 11.1: Landholding Percentages of Social Groups in Maharashtra

Division	Scheduled Caste		Scheduled Tribe		Others	
	Percentage of Holdings		Percentage of Holdings		Percentage of Holdings	
	Number	Area	Number	Area	Number	Area
Thane	2.51	2.03	30.64	42.98	66.85	54.98
Ahmednagar	7.59	6.62	5.52	6.54	86.89	86.84
Pune	4.26	3.55	5.30	7.09	90.43	89.36
Latur	6.42	5.52	1.33	1.28	92.25	93.19
Nanded	9.76	8.20	7.28	7.79	82.97	84.01
Akola	15.10	12.81	5.02	4.70	79.88	82.49
Vashim	12.07	10.24	4.88	4.93	83.05	84.83
Nagpur	9.86	9.35	5.80	6.45	84.34	84.19
State	**7.35**	**6.47**	**6.03**	**7.50**	**86.62**	**86.03**

Source: Computed from Agricultural Census, 2010-11.

area held by them is far lesser than the other categories. Even the Scheduled Tribe's position is better than the Scheduled Castes. The proportion of scheduled castes is high in marginal and small farmers' category while their proportion is less as the landholding size increases. Also compared to the general population, the proportion of scheduled Castes and Scheduled Tribes in agricultural labour is more. Approximately, 34 per cent of the agriculture labourers belong to the Scheduled Castes all over India, with regional variations. Punjab, Rajasthan and Uttar Pradesh have the highest percentage of Scheduled Castes agricultural labourers. the disproportionate landholding size is due to the denial of land to Dalits.

The problem of the Dalit and Adivasi landless agricultural labourers is grave in India. The problem is not only about landlessness, but also concerns the treatment meted out to them as labourers in the feudal set up of the agrarian society in India. Studies (Daniel & Alice Thorner, 2005; Bardhan and Rudra, 2003) have found that some of the traditional practices of exploitation still continue to persist under which services are taken from the labourers treating them as serfs. They are seldom paid wages. the traditional systems based on caste-based labour services appear to continue in the agrarian society. The persistence of the system of bonded labour in new forms and under new terminologies perpetuates humiliating conditions of labour in agrarian India, as most of the agricultural labourers are drawn from untouchable castes (Dhanagare, 1983; Omvedt, 1982). They bear the worst consequences of the deteriorating labour conditions. They hardly get wages in cash and if they demand reasonable wages according the fixed wages they are beaten up and atrocities committed against them. If they resist they are socially boycotted or often their women are raped. It is in this context that land rights are essential for the weaker sections so that they can lead a dignified life and escape discrimination in the agrarian society.

Land Reforms and Its Implications

The state had addressed the issues and concerns of the weaker sections with initiatives through land reforms. The main aim was to alter the relations based on land as it was thought that this would mitigate the problems of the weaker sections. The Kumarappa Committee of 1954 acknowledged the disparities in land holdings. The Committee stated that as many as 74.21 per cent of the landholders held only up to 5 acres which constituted 16.77 per cent of the total land. On the other hand 3.71 per cent of the landholders who held up to 25 acres or more held as much as 34.27 per cent of the total land (*Report of the Commission for Scheduled Castes and Scheduled Tribes*, April 1979-March 1980, Second Report, p. 20, Bhuskute, 2002). In order to alter the agrarian landholding structure, the state, through direct intervention, had undertaken reforms of land legislations and their implementation by government agencies. Social Action by pressure groups intervened directly for change in the agrarian structure in the form of peasant movements (Joshi, 1975: 87, Dhanagare, 1980: 14-15). These attempts to alter the agrarian structure directly can be characterised as land reforms (Joshi, 1975: 87).

Initially, the Indian National Congress took to transform the agrarian structure and raised the issue of *Zamindari* abolition and presented an agrarian reform programme in its Karachi and Faizpur sessions in 1931 and 1936 respectively. the Congress stood for land reforms to reduce rent and revenue of the collectors, the abolition of the *Zamindari* system and elimination of all intermediaries between the State and the cultivators (Malaviya, 1954: 27, 57-58, 62-64; Bhuskute, 2002: 46). A Planning Commission panel led by Gulzarilal Nanda later reviewed the progress of land reforms and made positive proposals that influenced the planners. Legislations were passed in different states between 1947 and 1952 that aimed at (a) abolition of intermediaries and absentee landlordism; and (b) providing security to the tenants by conferring occupancy rights upon them (Bhuskute, 2002; Dhanagare, 1980:14).

Dhanagare (1980) has reviewed the first phase of land reform legislation on the earlier accounts made by Daniel Thorner (1956), Doreen Warriner (1969), and P.C. Joshi (1971, 1976). The slogan in this phase was *land to the tiller*. In this phase of the land reforms, only the tenant and peasant land rights were taken up. Dhanagare (1980) pointed out that even though these reform measures led to the eviction of tenants, they were stifled by the landlords, as there were court cases pending, and no security was assured to the tenants and sharecroppers. He argued that the reform measures rather consolidated the rich landed classes as they got bulky compensation. But these reform measures largely ignored the problem of landless labourers, (Dhanagare, 1980:15-16). A majority of the landless were from the weaker sections and thus their land rights were ignored in the first phase.

The next phase of the land reforms concerned land ceiling measures. The objective of land ceiling was to ensure productivity by bringing more land under cultivation by involving landless persons in production by distributing them surplus land. The planners thought that this would bring to an end the land hunger and also give work and security to the landless. Thus the planners proposed steps to impose ceilings on existing agricultural holdings (Bhuskute, 2002; *Report of the Commissioner for Scheduled Castes and Scheduled Tribes*, April 1979-March 1980, Second Report, p. 26).

The federal structure of the Indian Union made it imperative that the ceiling measures were a state subject. Thus ceiling measures were contemplated in two phases in each state; in 1960 and in 1972. In the first phase, a survey of the land was undertaken, surplus land was estimated and cases were filed (*Report of the Commissioner for Scheduled Castes and Scheduled Tribes*, April 1979-March 1980, Second Report, p. 26; Bhuskute, 2002).

However, in the first phase of the ceiling measures, differences were found between the estimated surpluses, declared surplus and distributed surplus. For instance, in the Fifth Five-Year Plan, 1978-83 (as on 31-7-1977) the area estimated to be surplus was 53.20 lakh acres as against a declared surplus of 40.40 lakh acres. The area actually taken over by the government was a little more than one-half of the declared surplus (21.00 lakh acres) and the area actually distributed was only 12.90 lakh acres. On the other hand, the Ministry of Rural Reconstruction provides different figures. the estimated surplus amounted to 49.95 lakh acres while the declared surplus and the area taken over by the Government was 40.82 lakh acres and 24.90 lakh acres, respectively. The area distributed was 17.39 acres. The discrepancy in this data could be attributed to different standards adopted for assessing the surplus by the various states but the actual surplus seems to be more, taking into consideration the regional variations (*Report of the Commissioner for Scheduled Castes and Scheduled Tribes*, April 1979-March 1980, Second Report, p. 31).

The National Sample Survey (27th Round, 1971-72). declared a potential surplus as 215.10 lakh acres, while the Ministry of Rural Reconstruction had estimated the surplus of land at only 49.95 lakh acres. Thus, the estimated surplus was only a fraction of the area held in large ownership holdings as estimated from survey data (National Sample Survey, 27th Round, 1971-72). This data indicated that such discrepancy can be attributed to the fact that the surplus is computed on the basis of size of holdings; 10-18 acres with assured irrigation, 27 acres of land with irrigation for one crop and 54 acres for dry land. Also, the levels of ceiling differed in each state and for various categories of land (*Report of the Commissioner for Scheduled Castes and Scheduled Tribes*, April 1979-March 1980, Second Report: p. 31).

Thus, drastic measures were necessary to enforce land ceiling measures and to bring more land under the surplus land category. The Report further expressed its discontent that the estimated surplus was just a fraction of the area held in large ownership holdings (*Report of the Commissioner for Scheduled Castes and Scheduled Tribes*, April 1979-March 1980, Second Report, p. 31).

With reference to the estimated and actual declared surplus as per the figures given by the Ministry of Rural Reconstruction, out of 49,94,822 acres land estimated as surplus, the area declared as surplus in the country was 40,82,056 acres (81.72%) and area distributed was 17,39,339 acres (34.82%). The percentage of the area distributed and area declared surplus was 42.61 per cent. The Report thus shows that after the enactment of Land Ceiling Act, as much as 57.39 per cent of land declared surplus was not available to be allotted among the landless labourers. One of the possible reasons for land not being available for distribution was exemptions. The ceiling measures provided for exemptions on land being declared as surplus so as not to compromise the productivity. The following categories of land were qualified for exemption from ceiling:

- Sugarcane farms owned by sugar factories;
- Orchards;
- Plantation (tea, coffee and rubber);
- Special farms such as cattle breeding, dairy farms etc.;
- Farms in compact block;
- Efficient farms; and
- Mechanized farms and farms with heavy investment (*Report of the Commissioner for Scheduled Castes and Scheduled Tribes*, April 1979-March 1980, 2nd Report, pp. 27, 43).

Another reason was that the ceiling laws also set a deadline date for the landowners to declare their land holdings. This was the biggest constraint in the effective implementation of the amended legislation, i.e. a date with retrospective effect. It was pointed out that this enabled the big land-owners to deliberately effect transfers, partitions, sales, gifts etc., on a large scale with a retrospective date to overcome the National Guidelines, i.e. 24-1-1971, in anticipation of the ceiling legislation (*Report of the Commissioner for Scheduled Castes and Scheduled Tribes*, April 1979-March 1980, Second Report, p. 29).

Issues in the Implementation of Land Ceiling Measures and Exclusion of Weaker Sections

In order to assess the implementation of land ceiling measures and exclusion of weaker sections from land, the case of Maharashtra is presented in this section.

The Maharashtra Agricultural Lands (Ceiling and Holding) Act, 1961 came into force with effect from 26th January, 1962. Bhuskute (2002) points out that with the implementation of the ceiling law of 1961, only 1,25,000 hectares of land was available and the Maharashtra Government expected that due to the new amendment, another 1,50,000 hectares of land would be available. Thus, a total surplus land of 2,75,000 hectares was presumed to be available for distribution. Out of this, half of the land or so would be distributed among the landless, the Scheduled Castes and Scheduled Tribes. (Bhuskute, 2002: 74).

Bhuskute (2002) and Gopal Iyer (2002) point out that out of the estimated extent of land for distribution, a meagre area of about 3 per cent of the land was declared surplus compared to the total cultivable area and that too it was unproductive, inferior and barren (Bhuskute, 2002: 75; K. Gopal Iyer, 2002: 151). Gopal Iyer (2002) points out that there were talks between the bureaucrats and the landowners so that their land was not computed as surplus and that is why there was huge gap between the estimated and declared surplus and why the declared surplus was negligible (K. Gopal Iyer, 2002: 148). There was administrative laxity in computing the land holdings as the staff was inadequate, the definition of family was not proper, records were not up-to-date and moreover there were illegal transfers of land. This resulted in a large gap between the estimated surpluses and the actual declared surplus (K. Gopal Iyer, 2002: 148).

Bhuskute (2002) and K. Gopal Iyer (2002) point out that there were cases of circumvention using the provisions within the Ceiling Act so that the land owners could avoid their lands from being declared surplus. The landowners used various provisions like exemptions provided in the law, falsifying of records, and resorting to fictitious transfers etc. This was done in collusion with the *talatis* at Tehsil level (Bhuskute, 2002: 73; K. Gopal Iyer, 2002). Many landowners succeeded in changing the land classification to take advantage of the ceilings fixed for different categories of land. for instance, the ceiling for *jirayat* land was 54 acres, whereas for *bagayat* land the ceiling was 18 acres (Bhuskute, 2002: 75-76).

The date of declaration for transfer of land having been set by the government, the politicians who knew the effective date forewarned their kith and kin so that they could transfer their land in other's names. This deliberate act meant that the politicians were the main culprits in sabotaging the Land Ceiling measures (Bhuskute, 2002: 75-76). Bhuskute (2002) also points out that there was a rush of *Bargadars* to register deeds of partition, gift and transfers of holdings or partitions in the names of their kith and kins. Most of the transfers took place between 26th September, 1974 and 2nd October, 1975 to avoid the provision of the Act (K. Gopal Iyer, 2002: 151). Dhanagare also points out that there were *benami* transfers made between 1960 and 1970 on an unprecedented scale (Dhanagare, 1980: 17).

Gopal Iyer (2002) has pointed out that cases filed under *suo motu* administrative initiative related to big landowners. A number of cases were filed against big landowners and such cases took a long time to settle and release of the lands (K. Gopal Iyer, 2002: 157, 160-67). This brings out the fact that the ceiling measures were stifled by the big landowners and the land was retained in most of the cases. Bhuskute (2002) has argued that many transfers of land were made in contravention of the provision of Sections 8 and 9 of the Land Ceiling Act. He points out that the bureaucrats did not follow proper procedure laid down in the Land Ceiling Act due to lethargy, or even in collusion with the landlords and fudging of land records so that the landowners can save the land from being declared surplus (Bhuskute, 2002: 73). The bureaucrats were guilty as they helped the rich landowners to use the provisions of the Land Ceiling Laws in their favour.

The actual distribution of the surplus land was not satisfactory and there was no assistance after the landless were awarded lands. In some cases the original landholder did not hand over physical possession of the land as the fields were not surveyed and boundaries were not marked (Gopal Iyer, 2002: 168). Further, in many cases the lands distributed among the landless were not fit for cultivation and there were no irrigation facilities. Thus, there has been very marginal socio-economic impact on the beneficiaries (Gopal Iyer, 2002: 171-172).

As far as the distribution of land to the Scheduled Castes is concerned, the figures were not satisfactory. Citing land distribution data, Rajasekaran observes that it was moderate. K. Gopal Iyer (2002) also points out that some of the allottees from the Scheduled Castes were not given physical possession of the land. Rajasekaran (1998) finds that in spite of the reform measures, the Scheduled Castes and Scheduled Tribes continued to be deprived of land and inter-caste relations and caste domination remained the same. The Scheduled Castes and Scheduled Tribes beneficiaries were left without any support and facilities for cultivation like wells, agricultural implements, fertilizers, seeds etc. (Dhanagare, 1980:18) the politicians and bureaucrats are accused of working in collusion to deny land rights to the Scheduled Castes and that they saw to it that in the distribution of surplus land the first preference and better quality of land was given to the higher castes (Rajasekaran, 1998: 250). The bureaucratic control coupled with local leadership comprising the dominant castes, stifled the procedure to transfer land rights to Scheduled Castes as they could not reconcile to the fact that the Scheduled Castes were becoming cultivators. Therefore, the Land Ceiling measures stood largely defeated especially in the case of the Scheduled Castes.

Distribution of Government Waste Land/*Gairan* Land and Forest Land in Maharashtra

Distribution of government land to weaker sections formed the third phase of land reforms. There is no data with the Revenue and Forest Department about the extent of Government Waste Land/*Gairan* Land and Forest Land distributed to Dalits and Adivasis, though there had been distribution of government land in Maharashtra under the "Grow More Food Campaign". Government encouraged small and marginal farmers to encroach on government land for the purpose of cultivation and such encroachments were regularized (Bhuskute, 1989: 2355). Thus, the landless weaker sections started encroaching on government lands Also after the *Bhumiheen's* (landless) *Satyagraha*. The landless decided to eke out a living by cultivating government waste lands. (Bhuskute, 1989: 2255) the method of the *Satyagraha* was to take forceful possession of government waste land, *gairan* or forest land. As a response to the *Satyagraha*, Government Resolutions were issued for implementing the distribution of government waste land to Dalits and Adivasis.

Government Resolutions were issued by the Maharashtra Government from 1960 onwards (GR No. LEN 1069/23477-A-IID dated 14th August, 1972) to distribute government waste land to Dalits and Adivasis. The Government Resolutions were issued in two phases; from March 1960 to 1969 in the first phase and from 1972 onwards in the second phase. In second phase, forest, waste land and *gairan* were classified as lands meant for distribution. Government policy was notified by a GR issued in November 1991.

Implementation of the Government Resolutions: Inclusion or Exclusion

As pointed out by Bhuskute (1989), the government had no authentic and accurate figures regarding encroachments and the area of land under cultivation. In fact the encroachments by Dalits and Adivasis were strongly dealt with according to the Resolution of 1959. There was destruction of crops, forceful eviction of encroachers, fines, and prosecutions etc. But due to protests by Dalits and Adivasis through the *Bhumiheen's Satyagraha* and Kisan Sabha in Nasik and Thane, a GR dated 1 March, 1960 was issued by the Government of Maharashtra (Revenue and Forest Department) granting lands on a permanent basis in Vidarbha and Marathwada regions. *Eksali* cultivators were given first priority in the disposal of Government wastelands for cultivation, subject to the proviso that the land in the possession of the private as well as on *eksali* does not exceed one economic holding (Government Resolution, GR No. LND 3960-AI dated 1st March, 1960, Government of Maharashtra).

But, it was found that the GR was not seriously implemented by the bureaucrats (Bhuskute, 1989: 2256). Bhuskute points out that whatever distribution was done, it was done in a lethargic manner by the bureaucrats, who never left their tables. They did not indicate the exact boundaries, or the exact land allotted to the recipients, leading to a number of problems to the allottees.

The Government which initially allowed encroachments on its lands later changed its stand against encroachments (GR No. LND

1068/197549/A dated 23rd August, 1968) and decided in favour of eviction. But, it was only after the *Bhumiheen's Satyagraha*, that another GR was issued in March 1969 deciding that all the plot-holders who had been given plots on yearly basis would be allowed to keep such plots permanently. However, according to Bhuskute (1989) this decision was implemented only in Sholapur and that too after the Bombay High Court verdict in 1987. Thus the decision of GR of 1969 had not been implemented till 1989 although the Forest Department claims to have distributed 12,919.54 hectares to 4,872 plot-holders. The Maharashtra government had passed a resolution in July 1971 to give these plots to the tribals on permanent basis but was not completely or appropriately implemented.

Again, following the assertive action by landless Dalits and Adivasis, the Government was forced to take action in favour of encroachers. This was also due to improper implementation of the earlier resolutions and confusion over the problem of encroachments. Thus, the regularisation of the encroachment was done by GR No. LEN 1069/23477-A-IID, dated 14 August, 1972 following the *Bhumiheen's Satyagraha* which the GR itself acknowledged. The Government claimed that there has been substantial distribution of land to the landless. It also stated that there were encroachments by landless persons and government has issued circular to evict such encroachment even before the crops raised by them were harvested. In 1986, the Maharashtra Government gave the position after implementing the resolution of 12 September, 1979, about the number of legal and illegal encroachments (Bhuskute, 1989).

Table 11.2: Encroachment by Landless Persons

	Numbers	*Area (Hectares)*
Encroachments regularised	50192	80450
Encroachments not fit to be regularised	44220	59774
Pending Cases	10879	13335

Source: R.V. Bhuskute, *EPW*, 1989, p. 2356.

Bhuskute observes that the allotment of lands that were categorised as unfit for cultivation was decided arbitrarily without giving an opportunity to the plot-holder to establish its fitness for cultivation. According to Bhuskute, there were thousands of cases that do not figure in the government estimates. He further stated that there were 10-15 lakh illegal or authorised plot-holders of which the Dalits and Adivasis were in majority as per the government appointed High Power Committee (Bhuskute, 1989: 2355).

Again because of agitations by the Dalits and Adivasis, the Government decided to distribute government waste, *gairan* and forest lands to the landless encroachers in 1991. The Government of Maharashtra issued a GR (Revenue and Forest Department GR No. LEN-1090/PK/-172/G-1 dated 28th November, 1991) stating that even though there were GRs issued earlier for regularising the encroachments, more encroachments had taken place. It stated that an extent of 1,08,915.54 hectares of wasteland/*gairan* land was encroached by 84,230 persons between 1 April, 1978 and 14 April, 1990. This GR gave for the first time the official figures about the extent of encroachments, beneficiaries (backward classes and others) and allotted area (*see* Table 11.3).

The figures of encroachments that were given in this GR were very much less (Bhuskute, 1989). Thus, it is feared that a number of Dalit and Adivasi landless persons were left out from being recorded as encroachers. This had happened as the Dalits and Adivasis were denied the land. There were more encroachments that were identified later and subsequently GRs were issued by the government. GR No. LEN 1092/PK/65/G-1 dated 16 December, 1998 stated that there were pending cases for regularising and some unresolved cases of encroachment. The latter resolution, (GRNo. LEN/15/PK 40/G-1 dated 23 March, 1999) stated that cases from regularization was extended and some cases were pending and some remained unresolved even after the policy GR was drafted and orders passed in 1991. The GR stated that there were pending/unresolved cases in the government resolution (GR No. LEN 10/2001/PK 222/G-1, dated 14 August, 2001), and that such cases should be settled within 3 months by the Divisional Commissioner.

R.V. Bhuskute and K. Gopal Iyer have already assessed the implementation of the distribution of government lands in Maharashtra. As per Bhuskute (1989), most of these plot holders could not derive any benefit from the rightful ownership of these plots though their names are mentioned in the record of rights and also they have 7/12 extracts in their names. Government lands were distributed without ascertaining whether the land was fit for cultivation or not. The revenue officials assembled at the local *patwari's* residence/office or at the government rest house in the area and simply

Table 11.3: Details of Encroachments on Government Waste Land and *Gairan* Lands from 1st April, 1978 till 14th April, 1990

District	*Backward Class*	*Others*	*Total*	*Ares encroached in Hectares*		
				Wasteland	*Gairan*	*total Area*
Konkan Division						
Mumbai						
Mumbai Suburb						
Thane	1101	1220	2321	800.37	288.18	1088.55
Raigad	90	409	499	305.09	50.68	355.77
Ratnagiri	....	5	5	0.80	—	0.80
Sindhudurg	34	392	426	596.62	—	596.62
Total	1225	2026	3251	1702.88	338.83	2041.74
Nasik Division						
Nasik	111	75	186	147.82	109.73	257.55
Dhule	2069	613	2682	2900.40	2477.31	5377.71
Jalgaon	1073	715	1791	455.83	1545.58	2001.44
Ahmednagar	324	249	573	517.22	406.69	923.91
Total	3580	1652	5232	4021.30	4539.31	8560.61
Pune Division						
Pune	69	373	445	164.72	55.47	220.19
Sholapur	51	48	91	64.49	74.77	139.23
Satara	71	441	512	694.28	2.96	697.24
Sangli	—	13	13	—	8.38	8.38
Kolhapur	12	161	173	9.12	14.63	23.75
Total	203	1039	1242	932.61	156.21	1088.82
Nagpur Division						
Nagpur	311	192	503	340.52	196.92	537.44
Wardha	315	514	829	408.44	243.33	654.77
Chandrapur	11119	9187	20306	18150.00	26339.08	44489.08
Gadchiroli	3698	3036	6734	3295.67	2113.25	5408.92
Bhandara	4729	7938	12667	2723.06	3181.27	5904.33
Total	20172	20867	41039	24917.69	32073.85	56994.54
Amravati Division						
Amravati	1028	120	1148	—	1614.68	1614.68
Akola	1643	129	1772	153.89	1607.49	1761.30
Yavatmal	1350	368	1718	91.89	2517.42	2609.23
Buldhana	4326	564	4890	512.09	4830.46	5342.55
Total	8347	1181	9528	757.71	10570.05	11327.73

(*Contd. ...*)

District	Backward Class	Others	Total	Ares encroached in Hectares		
				Wasteland	Gairan	total Area
Aurangabad Division						
Aurangabad	3321	1037	4358	26.37	4533.55	4559.92
Beed	1932	106	2038	—	2405.74	2405.74
Nanded	7651	2125	9776	—	12989.04	12989.04
Parbhani	3489	438	3927	—	4601.53	4601.53
Osmanabad	95	18	113	1.17	111.14	112.31
Jalna	2107	226	2333	—	2658.50	2658.50
Latur	1257	136	1393	—	1575.00	1575.00
Total	**19852**	**4086**	**23938**	**27.54**	**28874.53**	**28902.07**
All Total	**53371**	**30851**	**84230**	**32359.73**	**73555.89**	**108915.54**

Source: Government of Maharashtra, Revenue and Forest Department Government Resolution No. LEN-1090/PK/-172/G-1 dated 28th November, 1991.

made the necessary changes in the village records and in the record of rights. Thus, uncultivable waste lands were distributed. The lands distributed were not surveyed properly, no boundaries were marked nor the areas demarcated, and maps of this land and *Kami Jasti Patraks* were prepared. Thus, the revenue officers registered all these plots under the government land again that has been distributed to the tribals and Dalits on the pretext of the absence of the *Kami Jasti Patrak* (Bhuskute, 1989: 2357).

K. Gopal Iyer (2002) has pointed out that there were violations of norms for allotment of land. For instance, as per the norms of allotment, priority has to be given to weaker sections of the society comprising of scheduled caste and scheduled tribes. In his study it was found, on an average, amongst the beneficiaries 28.50 per cent were SC and 24.50 per cent were ST and the rest 47 per cent were from other castes. He pointed out that around 41.83 per cent of lands had been allotted to SC and 19.74 per cent to ST at the state level. There were violations up to 64 to 100 per cent in the allotment of lands to other castes. His study revealed that out of the total encroachers, 83 per cent belonged to the non-SC and ST castes. His study also revealed that the dominant land owning community was the major encroacher on government land. the study pointed that the regularization of encroachments was contrary to the objective of distribution of land to the weaker sections as a large number of beneficiaries belonged to the upper castes.

Bhuskute (1989) had rightly argued that this shows how the government has played with the weaker sections in the distributing land rights by making weak resolutions. He alleges that framing weak policies and issuing manoeuvrable resolutions were the tactics adopted by the government to evict Dalits and Adivasis from the government and forest lands respectively. Thus the methods used by government amounted to deceit and fraud on the one hand and at times resorting to generosity and muscle power to drive off the landless Dalits and Adivasi from the lands (Bhuskute, 1989: 2355). The question of land rights of Dalits and Adivasis has become very important issue as there was no proper implementation of the government resolutions and they were deprived of their land. Thus, there were state level protests and demonstration for land rights and protection to the landless labourers in various parts of Maharashtra by Dalits and Adivasis.

Conclusion

The state has an important role to play in altering relationships in an agrarian society. Mounting pressure from various social movements (peasant movements) has impacted so much that the state had to resort to implement land reforms. It has attempted to undertake the land reforms to alter the agrarian relationship. But, during the process of implementation, the reforms have not only led to the eviction of tenants but also to the consolidation of their position in the agrarian society by the landlords. the issue of land distribution to landless weaker sections was initiated by various State Governments with land ceiling measures. This was initiated due to various protest movements by the agriculture labourers in India and especially due to pressure from the *Bhumiheen's Satyagraha* that was spearheaded under the Dalit movement. It is because of the impact of this *Satyagraha* that priority was given to distribution of surplus land to agricultural labourers belonging to the Scheduled Castes and Scheduled Tribes. In the first phase of the ceiling imposed on land holdings, a huge gap appeared between the estimated surplus and declared surplus, which could be attributed to not only to administrative laxity but also to the fact that the big landowners could manage to evade their land from being declared surplus in collusion with bureaucrats and loopholes in the law. The class interest among the bureaucrats, land owners and politicians brought them together in an unholy alliance to circumvent the ceiling on land holdings. They stifled and sabotaged the ceiling measures as it went against their caste-class interests. Implementation of the ceiling measures lacked political will and thus remained a little more than a paper exercise. As a result, upper caste domination was consolidated in rural areas as there was no physical handing over of the land distributed to Scheduled Castes and Scheduled tribes. With regard to the distribution of government lands, there was more bureaucratic lethargy in the process of distribution of land to Dalits and Adivasis. In fact the Dalits and Adivasis were driven out of their rightful possession of these lands by the dominant sections in rural areas with bureaucratic connivance. In a majority of the cases, encroachments on government lands by Dalits and Adivasis were not seen as fit cases for regularisation. Though, some of the Dalits and Adivasis got lands (where the Dalit and Adivasi movement was strong) and their land *pattas* were regularized, a majority of the encroachers on the government waste lands were denied their due on account of large scale violation of the programme in Maharashtra.

To conclude, the bureaucratic institutions have been used by the upper echelons from the rural rich to stifle the land distribution programmes. This brings out that institutions (especially bureaucratic) become discriminatory and non-inclusive as the dominant sections have a nexus with them (as they have similar class-caste interests). Though the 'state' has committed to the inclusion of Dalits and Adivasis, in reality large sections amongst them remain excluded from land possessions.

References

Agricultural Census, 2010-11.

Bardhan, Pranab with Ashok Rudra (2003) "Types of Labour Attachment in Agriculture," in Pranab Bardhan (Ed.), *Poverty, Agrarian Structure, and Political Economy in India,* New Delhi : Oxford University Press.

Bhuskute, R.V. (1989), Tribals, Dalits and Government Lands, in *Economic and Political Weekly*, Vol. 24, Issue No. 42.

Bhuskute, R.V. (2002), "Overview of Land Reforms in India", In Ghanshyam Shah and D. C. Sah (Eds.), *Land Reforms in India,* Volume 8, New Delhi : Sage Publications.

Daniel and Alice Thorner. (2005), *Land and Labour in India.* New Delhi : Chronicle Books.

Deshpande, R.S. (2002), "Land Reforms and Agrarian Structure in Maharashtra", in Ghanshyam Shah and D.C. Sah (Eds.), *Land Reforms in India,* Volume

8, New Delhi : Sage Publications.

Dhanagare, D.N. (1982), *Rural Transformation in India: Challenges and Prospects*, J S.S. Institute of Economic Research, Dharwad, 1982.

Gopal Iyer, K. (2002), "Implementation of the Land Ceiling Act in Western India," in Ghanshyam Shah and D.C. Sah (Eds.), *Land Reforms in India,* Volume 8, New Delhi : Sage Publications.

Government of India, *Report of the Commission for Scheduled Castes and Scheduled Tribes*, April 1979-March 1980, Second Report.

Government of Maharashtra (1962), *Land Ceiling Law in Maharashtra*, Bombay, May 1962.

Joshi, P.C. (1975), *Land Reforms in India,* Delhi : Allied Publishers.

Malaviya, H.D. (1954), *Land Reforms In India,* Delhi : National Printing Works.

Rajasekaran, N. (1998), "Land Reforms in Maharashtra: A Regional Analysis", *Review of Development and Change*, III/II, July-December.

12

Gender Budgeting for Urban Local Bodies to Make Cities Gender-Friendly

Vibhuti Patel

Introduction

One of the basic features of Good Governance should be women's empowerment and creating conditions for gender equality. No government can claim to be working in the best interests of its population if it ignores women, who normally constitute 50 per cent of the population. Of course, there is no dearth of governments proclaiming their women-friendly policies. Where they fail is in the implementation of such proclaimed policies. The Women's Policy Document, 2013 of the Maharashtra State government, for example, states emphatically:

> "Gender budgeting is essential so that the principles of men-women equality, eradication of gender-based discrimination and gender equality are reflected boldly in the planning of all departments of the state. This would help improve women's contribution in economy, make opportunities to earn available to them, capacity building of women, improve their educational and vocational eligibility, ensure better health for women and increase political participation and social status of women" (Women's Policy, 2013, Women and Child Development Department, Government of Maharashtra).

The policy document asks every department of the State government to define its programmes, draft policies and formulate schemes in order to improve women's social status and establish men-women equality in political, social, economic and cultural spheres. the departments are asked to make funds available for the schemes, implement and evaluate them. The overall responsibility of following up the gender budget and implementation of it is entrusted to the State's Women's Commission or equivalent institute.

This chapter discusses the various aspects of gender budgeting by Urban Local Bodies (ULBs).

Guidelines for Preparation of Gender Budgeting

In the broadest sense, budgeting or formulation of a budget is not merely limited to the preparation of a document of financial outlay. It involves a series of actions and processes that precede the preparation of the budget as well as the events and processes that follow it. It is a continuing process. The urban local self-government bodies are provided a policy framework, methodology and set of tools to enable them integrate a gender perspective into their annual budget. The urban local bodies have to integrate gender budgeting in their Annul Plan, Annual Financial Statement, Budget Estimates, Performance Budget (department-wise) etc.

Definition of Gender Budgeting

Gender Budgeting may be defined as a process that requires looking at the budget from a gender perspective to assess how it addresses the needs of women in specific areas. It does not mean the creation of a separate budget for women, but seeks affirmative action to address the specific requirements of women. Gender Budgeting is, in fact, a tool for assessing the impact of Government revenue and expenditure on women and covers areas such as policy review, assessment of needs, programme formulation, resource allocation, implementation, assessment of impact, reprioritisation of resources etc. A gender sensitive budget is the result of this process.

Tools for Gender Budgeting

Besides the indicators for gender budgeting mentioned above, what is more important is the assessment of the needs of the beneficiary and impact analysis. It should also include spatial mapping—micro-level planning for micro-level needs. Mere allocation of funds in the budget is not enough unless gender concerns are kept in view. These will have to include:

- Curbing diversion of kerosene from the Public Distribution System;
- Keeping a gender perspective while rationalising interest subsidy on account of small savings, especially postal savings like National Savings Scheme;
- Conducting a gender sensitive review of the incidence of taxes;
- Regulation of interest rates in micro-credit sector;
- Provision social security to women through insurance, SHGs, low interest credit facilities; and
- Increasing women's participation in sports through scholarships, hostels, training/practice facilities.

Visibility of Women in Statistics and Indicators

It is important for ULBs to arrange gathering data in such a way as to make visibility of women in statistics and indicators. The data-base must throw light on the gap between women and men in critical areas like economic participation, economic opportunity, political empowerment, educational attainment, and health. These categories identify the concrete measures required to be taken to reduce the gender gap and provide an unambiguous framework for future policy-making and gender budgeting. Gender sensitive analysis of budgets has to take into account the following:

- Gender awareness in policy appraisal;
- Beneficiary assessments;
- Gender disaggregated public expenditure incidence analysis;
- Gender disaggregated tax incidence analysis;
- Gender disaggregated analysis of the impact of the budget on time-use;
- Gender awareness in medium term economic policy framework; and
- Gender aware budget framework.

Composition and Functioning of Gender Budget Cells (GBCs)

The Gender Budget Cell should comprise a cohesive group of senior/ middle level officers from the various departments of the ULBs like Planning, Policy, Coordination, Budget and Accounts. This group should be headed by a senior officer and its functions and working reviewed periodically. The GBC may set for itself specific targets to be achieved in terms of the following areas of work:

- Identification of 3 to 6 largest programmes (in terms of budget allocation) for implementation by the ULB with a view to conducting an analysis of the gender issues addressed by them. Output indicators may be identified for measurement against performance in the next year.
- Highlight the activities targeted at improving the situation of women under these programmes; assess the adequacy of budget allocation; and monitor the expenditure and whether the benefits are delivered and to whom. It is also necessary to assess whether the policy as implemented has changed the situation in promoting/achieving greater gender equality.
- Departments with Gender Budgeting have to conduct a performance audit (at the field level wherever possible) for reviewing the achievement of physical/financial targets and identify the constraints so as to strengthen the delivery systems, infrastructure/capacity building etc.
- The departments should get a feedback on the efficacy of sectoral policies and programmes through meetings/discussions/consultations with the related departments within the ULB, elected women representatives, field level organisation/civil society groups/NGOs working in the sector etc.
- As "gender neutral" programmes need not necessarily be gender neutral in their impact on women. Urban Development, PWD, Power, Telecom, Communications, Transport and Industry etc. may also identify the initiatives/special measures to facilitate/improve access to services for women and their active participation in the decision making process at various levels.
- It would be advisable to disseminate the best practices followed any particular Division/Department/ULB etc., in implementing schemes, among others.

There are other areas in which actions are required to be taken in the interests of women. These include:

- Providing social security and protection to women construction workers;
- Creating ward-wise counselling centres and halfway homes/ drop-in centres for senior citizens, women in slums, commercial sex workers, rag pickers, domestic helps, street children (girls);
- Establishing crisis prevention centres and shelter homes for women survivors of violence besides working women's hostels, public toilets and rest rooms at bus stations and railway stations;
- Enacting a comprehensive Food Security Bill with universal PDS as a component;
- Allocating 6 per cent each of the total outlay of the ULB for Health and Education;
- Increased allocation for women farmers, tribal, dalit, and minority women; and
- Support for schemes for women-headed households and differently abled women.

Gender Budgeting in Urban LSG Bodies

The process of gender budgeting demands special programmes targeting women based on enumeration of differential impact of expenditures across all sectors and services; gender disaggregated impact on literacy, school drop-outs, mortality, morbidity, malnutrition, illnesses, safety and security. Hence, there is a need to ensure a review of equal opportunity policies and opportunities in public sector-jobs, school education, wages, health care, skills, technical training, and computer education.

Allocation and Utilisation of Resources for Women in ULB Budgets

NIPFP has recommended the following classification of financial allocation on schemes and programmes for gender audit as well as gender budgeting:

- Women specific schemes where 100 per cent of the allocation is required to be spent on women targeted 100 per cent to women by Ministry of Women and Child Development (MWCD).

- Pro-women schemes, where at least 30 per cent of the allocation and benefit flows to women, e.g. all anti-poverty programmes;
- Gender Neutral Schemes meant for the community as a whole (Employment Generation Programmes, Jawaharlal Nehru National Urban Renewal Mission); and
- Residual schemes for disaster management.

Besides giving details of all schemes under the above 4 categories through its publications, workshops and training programmes, the All India Institute of Local Self-Government also trains the elected representatives in efficient ways of programme implementation through budgeting from below.

Budgetary Allocation for Protective and Welfare Services

These are schemes that directly benefit women in situations arising out of economic and socio-cultural subordination and de-humanisation and include shelter homes, short stay homes, rehabilitation schemes for women survivors of violence, pensions for and widows and destitute.

Budgetary allocations for Social Services Expenditure is aimed at capacity building by way of reduction of domestic drudgery and affording better quality of life for girls and women and include: (a) Housing, Education, Health and Nutrition; (b) Working women's hostels and Crèches; (c) Water supply, Sanitation, Toilets, Drainage; and (d) Fuel, Waste Management and Transport. Budgetary allocations for Economic Services to provide economic opportunities to women include:

- SHGs-credit, loans to self-employed women, training programmes, vocational training in biotechnology, IT etc.;
- Physical infrastructure (transport, energy);
- Reservation of 10 per cent flats/tenements for single women in urban areas;
- Marketing facilities for women entrepreneurs and self-employed women: reserving 10 per cent of shops for businesswomen, women vendors/traders in municipal markets, women's *haats*/bazaars;
- Public toilets for women without user fees; and

- Safe and efficient transport for working women and women vendors.

Budgetary allocation for Regulatory Services has to be made for putting in place institutional structures and mechanisms like:

- State/Municipal Commission for Women;
- Women Development Cells in municipal bodies, police stations, LSG offices, municipal hospitals and schools;
- Budgetary allocation and space for ward-wise WDC for prevention of sexual harassment of women in the organised and unorganised sectors; and
- Awareness generation programmes.

State Governments must devolve substantive powers, funds, functions and functionaries upon LSG bodies. Similarly, the Central Government should strive for simplification of programme guidelines regarding women specific schemes. Moreover, Centrally Sponsored Schemes could be recast to empower municipal bodies. PRIs must get untied funds to formulate plans according to their needs and priorities. Structures and mechanisms for RTI Act must be put in place to sort out problems concerning utilisation of funds. To avoid urban unrest and guarantee socio-economic justice, at least 100 days of employment at minimum wages must be provided under EGS in all urban centres.

Financial Matters and ULBs

Besides having adequate powers in matters relating to gender mainstreaming, the ULBs should also ensure that they exercise such powers, especially in:

- Adopting mechanisms to analyse budgetary policies through gender lens;
- Monitor the implementation of women-centric schemes and control significant deviation between Budget Estimates and Revised Estimates;
- Separate listing of women specific items and women's component and transparency in utilisation of the allocated amount for women's programmes;

- Segregation and introduction of transparency in the budget to protect diversion of provisions earmarked for women especially under health, education and rural development;
- Developing strategic gender tools to monitor implementation and impacts;
- Conduct Benefit Incidence Analysis to know whether the budgetary allocations have benefited the targeted beneficiaries;
- Increase and prepare new schemes for grant-in-aid support for women's resource centres;
- Involve elected women in ULBs in the formulation of budgets so as to avoid disjunction between planning and budget that would on the one hand exclude women and on the other hand make the budget exercise totally centralized, with priorities and schemes that are not rooted in local government needs;
- Increase women's participation in economic decision making by promulgating a percentage representation in all sectors where revenue and expenditure is being decided, including finance commissions and taxation reform commissions (women economists and women developmental experts who understand the impact of development on men and women must be part of this as well as a gender expert to be on these committees); and
- Strengthen the gender-disaggregated database within relevant Departments so as to enable an effective monitoring of targets and achievements across gender.

An Important Challenge

The target of 30 per cent gender allocations in all poverty alleviation and development oriented schemes and programmes have not yet been achieved as per the promise of women component plan (WCP) of Government of Maharashtra in 2005. This must be implemented immediately. There is a need for gender audit and gender outcome appraisal of all departments at the Central and State levels. Very often, resource allocations made under gender budgeting do not reach in time and they remain unspent. There should be proper monitoring and supervision of the allocated funds with greater transparency and accountability at all levels.

References

Bandopadhyaya, D. (2002) "Panchayats in Karnataka". *Economic and Political Weekly,* 37(35): 3572-3573.

Banerjee, N. "What is gender budgeting? Public policies from women's perspective in the Indian context", *United Nations Development Fund for Women*, Delhi, (Available at http://www.unifem.org.in)

Banerjee, N. and Roy, P. (2004) "What Does the State do for Indian Women?" *Economic and Political Weekly, Review of Women Studies,* XXXIX (44): 4831-4837.

Bhatt, A., Kolhar, S., Chellappa, A. and Anand, H. (2004) "Building Budgets from Below", Mumbai. *Economic and Political Weekly, Review of Women Studies,* XXXIX (44): 4803-4810.

Budget 2017-18: Dream or Despair? Response to the Union Budget, 2007-08, Centre for Budget and Governance Accountability (CBGA), Delhi, 2017.

Lahiri, A., Chakraborty, L and Bhattacharya, P.N. (2002) *Gender Budgeting in India*, National Institute of Public Finance and Policy, New Delhi.

Nakray, K. (2009) *Gender budgeting: Does it really work? Some Experiences from India.* U.K.: Policy and Politics, the Policy Press, 37(2), pp. 307-10.

Patel, V. (2002) *Women's Challenges of the New Millennium,* Delhi : Gyan Books.

Patel, V. (2009) *United Nations Development Fund for Women and the Commonwealth Secretariat.* (Available at http://www.gender-budgets.org/content/view/292/156/)

Rajaram, I. (2007). *Women in the Eleventh Plan*, National Institute of Public Finance and Policy, New Delhi.

Sahu, S. (2002) *Decentralised financial and physical planning: A study Across Gram Panchayats and Blocks in Midnapore District of West Bengal.* Department of Economics, with Rural Development, Vidyasagar University, West Bengal.

UNDP, (2001) *Decentralisation in India: Challenges and Opportunities*, United Nations Development Programme, New Delhi.

13

Interrogating Modi's Leadership Style

The Demonetisation Debate

Manisha Madhava

Introduction

As the debate on demonetisation continues, an important aspect of demonetisation, i.e. the nature of Modi's leadership has received inadequate attention. The events leading to demonetisation and those following it bring to fore Prime Minister Narendra Modi's style of leadership more clearly than ever before. Modi's leadership comes across in stark contrast to that of his predecessor, Dr. Manmohan Singh who was more a quiet and reticent leader.

The BJPs 2014 election campaign had portrayed Narendra Modi as decisive and experienced leader. He further added to his imagery through slogans such as *Sab ka Saath, Sab ka Vikas*, which gave the impression that he was a collaborative and accommodating leader. His charismatic appeal, coupled with the lack of an alternative leadership, led to the BJP emerging as the single largest party in the Lok Sabha, a feat not achieved by any other party since 1991.

Narendra Modi's political journey is marked by several milestones, each one of which tells us something about his political style. Though this style is continuously evolving and has recreated several times in the course of the term, certain elements of the leadership style are deeply entrenched. Events like the surgical strikes against Pakistan and demonetisation give us a glimpse of the core of Modi's leadership style—strategic leadership.

There can be no doubt about the fact that Demonetisation of 1000 and 500 Rupee notes, which constituted nearly 86 per cent of the country's currency was a bold decision. It would most definitely have an impact on the average man on the street, who was Modi's greatest vote bank and who had in large numbers supported Modi in the 2014 election. Modi chose disruptive methods over gradual incremental changes to usher in what he believed would bring about transformation of the country's economy. At risk were his entire support base and his political future. No one is sure of the extent to which the finance minister or other cabinet members were privy to this move. The country remains in the dark about whose counsel the Prime Minister had sought while firming up this most drastic and draconian change in currency notes. Despite the odds, the government decided to take a call indicating Modi's appetite for risk taking. But, this was an act of faith; strategised meticulously to minimise his losses, at the outset.

Announcing the Decision

The timing and the manner in which the announcement was made are both significant. Modi chose to announce the decision through a televised address to the nation. It is not unusual for leaders to address the nation on important occasions. But, an out of turn televised address adds seriousness to the matter, which Modi wanted. His initial announcement was so powerful and energetic that it carried popular opinion. The media was fully on his side and a nervous Congress lacking in confidence also announced support for the move. Only two grassroots leaders, Mamata Banerjee and Arvind Kejriwal, recognised the danger and opposed it. It is difficult to imagine the Manmohan Singh government producing this kind of euphoria in either the media or the middle class urban population if it had chosen to demonetize.

Interestingly, the announcement was made on 9th of November; a week before the session of the parliament was to commence. The timing of this 'surgical strike' was planned, perhaps, to catch the opposition unawares, which has been gearing up the attack the government in the Parliament, in view of the Assembly elections.. The demonetisation was sure to give the opposition enough ammunition. The timing of the decision reveals that he wished to weather and face the brunt of the early attacks. The government believed that by the time the parliamentary session was convened, the early inconvenience from the move would be mitigated and things would be limping back to normalcy; or so the government thought. The announcement was also ahead of the upcoming State elections in five important states, where BJP had high stakes. To limit the impact of the decision, were it be negative, the announcement came well ahead of the elections, but not immediately so.

Communicating the Decision

An interesting aspect of Modi's leadership style has been the use of the media. Not only did Modi get direct with the people through his radio broadcast *Mann Ki Baat,* but also through various channels of communication. The traditional rallies and speeches apart, he is one of the few leaders to make extensive use of the social media; the Twitter and Facebook. During the entire fortnight Modi has not only been active on social media, but also gone a step ahead and commenced a virtual referendum on his Facebook page. There were over five lakh responses to his 'referendum' on the first day of its launch. The direct communication with the masses bypassing the traditional institutions such as the parliament is a double edged sword. While Modi continues to awe and inspire many, he is fettered by criticisms and checks from the institutional mechanisms such as the Parliament. This has given him ample room to manoeuvre his responses and fine tune his strategy.

Language of Discourse

In his televised address, Modi sought support of his "countrymen" to get rid of the menace of black money the move was touted as one of countering black marketing and corruption, a scourge that most Indian's feel is the bane of the country's progress and was likely to receive public support. While there may have been many other considerations that led the government to the decision, Modi chose to highlight the corruption aspect, among others. The discourse was couched in nationalist language. It seemed to imply that patriotic Indians would and should support (any) move to rid the country of graft. The language used was emotive and a surcharged atmosphere was created through extensive use of social media. In fact, in the past too, the BJP's use of social media to garner support has been exemplary.

Leading From the Front

Once the decision was announced, Modi directed things from the forefront. Regular cabinet meetings were held to review the implementation of the decision and damage control, in the form of raising withdrawal limits, use of indelible ink, concessions on withdrawal limits for farmers and families with marriages, was announced. Parliamentarians were asked to return to their constituencies over the week-end and communicate the benefits of the move. Modi himself addressed at least four rallies in different part of the country on his return to India to justify the decisions.

Manoeuvring the Discourse

Modi said that normalcy would not return before 50 days. With this second move, he bought himself time and space to recalibrate his strategy. It is this comment on 50 days of inconvenience that allowed him the freedom to think of how to re-position demonetisation. There was no reference to a digital economy in his initial announcement, which was limited to black money, counterfeit currency and terrorism. It was only after his return from Japan that the discourse suddenly shifted because of Modi's talent and credibility. One can picture him thinking about it alone. The opposition said this was a shifting of goalposts, but they should understand that this is not a university debate. So long as Modi can convince large sections of the population that the policy is good and the inconvenience will ultimately be beneficial, he will continue to do so. the specific benefits of the policy are unimportant to politics. Proof of this appeared when the Bharatiya Janata Party continued its electoral successes across India even a month after demonetisation, including in Punjab where it was in power and suffering anti-incumbency. There is actually no opposition to Modi at the moment and he is still in full control of the narrative, which is astonishing because it has affected every single Indian negatively.

Disarming the Opposition

A lacklustre opposition immediately got a shot in its arm and took no time to criticize and debunk the government. Mamata Banerjee of the Trinamool Congress took the lead and Kejriwal of the Aam Admi Party soon joined the bandwagon. While other opposition parties and even the allies of BJP like the Shiv Sena criticized the government, their impact fell short. The opposition was unable to forge a joint front and the fractures within it were wide open. The Congress refused to join ranks with the TMC and the AAP. The reasons were technical; Mamata wanted a roll back, while Congress wanted to reduce the hardship caused to the common man. Even within the ranks of the Congress party, there emerged different voices. While Rahul Gandhi relied on optics and stood in the queue to withdraw Rs. four thousand P. Chidambaram, the former Finance Minister gave a more nuanced criticism. A reticent Manmohan Singh launched a frontal attack on the government, criticizing its policy, calling it legalised loot and plunder. However, given the language in which the discourse was couched, the opposition could not challenge the decision of the government effectively.

Within the Parliament both the government and opposition adopted an obdurate stand. The opposition wanted a debate in the Parliament under rule 53 which allows for voting at the end of it, while the government refused to debate the demonetisation under the rule. The government accused the opposition of refusing the debate, while the opposition alleged the BJP was reluctant to field the Prime Minister and face censure of the House. The net result was the complete washout of the winter session of the Parliament. Modi did participate in the debates in the Lok Sabha, while he continued to address the nation through public rallies, meetings and direct radio broadcast of his address to the people.

Conclusion

That Narendra Modi is an inspirational leader was evident during the election campaign itself. His political slogans and campaign strategy gave a glimpse of the reasons behind his political appeal which led to the BJP capturing power at the centre on its own. The demonetisation imbroglio has brought forth certain other facets of his leadership style which hitherto were discussed only behind the scenes and by those who worked in close proximity to him. For one, in Narendra Modi's style of leadership, decisions are driven by the leadership. Individuals and institutions merely influence and streamline the decisions from the margins. This style leads to fast and effective decision making, but lacks the power of collective wisdom. Further, since the decisions are not collaborative, the success or the failure of the decision is also individual. fortunately for Modi, he has not yet faced any major reverses and has for most part received accolades. Secondly, transformative decisions are leadership driven. They have to be strategically implemented and executed and in this task Modi's methodical approach and frontal leadership are clearly evident.

While these are valuable traits in a leader, these very traits can create the way for authoritarianism, especially if there are little or no institutional checks. Herein lies the challenge for Narendra Modi; to provide a strong leadership that the nation yearns without either jeopardizing the institutional backbone or democratic fabric. For now, the challenge to Narendra Modi comes from Narendra Modi!

14

Political Leadership and Ethics

The Case of Gandhiji and Raychandbhai

Arpita Shah

Introduction

The essay on "Political Leadership and Ethics: the Case of Gandhiji and Raychandbhai" has been written primarily to coincide with two events—one, the forthcoming 150th birth anniversary of Mahatma Gandhi in 2019 and second, Raychandbhai's (henceforth Param Krupalu Dev) 150th birth anniversary in 2017.

Rabindranath Tagore wrote in *Modern Review* of September 1934:

> "...success in a conflict may be terrible defeat from the human point of view, and material gain is not worth the price we pay at spiritual cost. Much rather should we lose all than barter our soul for an evil victory. We honour Mahatma Gandhi because he has brought this ideal into the sphere of politics..." (Bhattacharya, 2014:203).

Speaking of 'moral warfare' in the same article, Tagore, India's one of the finest poets, had credited Gandhiji for reminding humanity of the ideals of Truth and *Ahimsa* in fighting against the evil of untruth between countries as one fights for a '*dharma yuddha*'.

Gandhiji's greatest contribution, more than striving for the country's independence, as the world regards, has been the tools with which he fought for '*Poorna Swaraj*'. He has been acknowledged and reckoned the world over as one leading an ethical life. His search for 'Truth', self-realization, self-discipline and strong spiritual inclination in the most minute and mundane activities reflects the depth of his desire to lead a righteous life.

It is quite an achievement for a politician of this day and age to abide by the virtues astutely and strictly, irrespective of the changing seasons or conditions of health and without any favour or ill-will towards anyone. Gandhiji, who walked on the same land as we do, just about a hundred and fifty years back, not too long a period in history, on the other hand, showcased how consistent persistence at bringing true welfare to the masses through strength and purity in purpose and means to achieve them, uplifts and awakens not just those who are deprived, but also oneself and the humanity at large.

His pursuit and achievements beget many questions: What was the source of Gandhiji's 'experiments with truth'? How did the transformation from a Mohandas who believed meat eating would give the country independence to a 'Mahatma' who was perennially fasting and left no stone unturned for self-sacrifice, take place? How did ethics help him mould his character? How did that help him lead the struggle for freedom?

Gandhiji's autobiography '*My Experiments with Truth*' reveals that there were three main influences: Tolstoy's "*The Kingdom of God is within You*", Ruskin's "*Unto this Last*" and Raychandbhai. Amongst them, Raychandbhai or Shrimad Rajchandra (or *Aram Krupalu Dev* as he was later called) had a lasting impression on account of Gandhiji's personal acquaintance.

'*Yugpurush*', a highly gripping play inspired by Shrimad Rajchandra Mission, Dharampur under the guidance of *Pujya Gurudev* Shri Rakeshbhai, very lucidly explains this metamorphosis. It is a revelation of the relationship between two great souls: Gandhiji and *Aram Krupalu Dev*, his mentor.

Having been inspired by the play, this essay has for its objective to understand the centrality of ethics in the life of a political leader. What it ultimately infers is that ethics is the cornerstone of Good Governance. An ethical society, a society that is grounded in morality and virtues, that puts a premium over spiritual and moral health of its citizens, resolves problems of discord and disharmony in a way that is more evolved and welfare-enhancing. Since the State is composed of a multitude of stake holders, an ethical State would include all of them in its ambit. The idea here is not of the fantasy of a utopian state but one, where, in spite of problems emanating from free-riding and negative externalities exist a higher priority on democratic living in its truest sense. If it does so, the transaction costs of resolving the social disruptions turn out to be lower. Minus ethics, the founding pillars of democracy are absent and there is high susceptibility to barbarity, let alone governance of any kind.

Gandhiji and Aspects of His Political Leadership

Ethics or 'moral philosophy' as we know, doesn't seem to be a narrative only of do's and the don'ts (Thompson, 1999:3). In fact, if morality means to do the righteous, what comes to rescue is the knowledge of what is 'ought not to be done'. the means to know what is righteous comes from what gives eternal happiness. It is this 'Perfect Righteousness' that gives happiness and the ancient Indian scriptures are a proof to this. What this entails is, to for ever seek the 'Truth' since that alone gives the soul happiness it pines for.

Gandhiji was one such seeker, pining to realise the self, striving to realise the eternal principles of 'Truth'. If Godliness is the exalted state of happiness, he rightly thus said of God as Truth and in realising this inner calling, he could see how service to mankind was taking him closer to Godhood. At the service of animal care, he wrote in *Harijan* on March 11, 1939: "All the twenty four hours of the day, I am with the dumb millions. They are my first care and last, because I recognise no God except the God that is to be found in the hearts of the dumb millions" (Desai, 2001:87). A sense of service, by default, calls for love and selfless service calls for unconditional love.

Accounts of his life give an impression that more than an intended thought of being a leader, compassion and sympathy made him one. Politics happened to be a channel of or an instrument for illuminating lives of millions in utter despair. Gandhiji writes: "I cannot isolate politics from the deepest things of my life, for the simple reason that my politics are not corrupt, they are inextricably bound up with Non-violence and Truth" (Desai 2001: 41).

Born on 2nd October, 1869, through all the literature available we know the Mahatma as a child to be shy, truth loving, inherently virtuous and someone who in spite of the many fallacies of the youth and ignorance emphasized on development of character. Whether it was the inspector who tried to persuade a seven year old into copying the word 'kettle' or the guilt pangs of having eaten meat, stealing coppers from the servants for smoking, attempt at suicide or the incidents of carnal desires Gandhiji mentions in his autobiography, there is an honest revelation and a strong sense of accountability to the self.

The promises he made to his mother before going to England, at the insistence of Becharji Swami, a family adviser that he would not touch 'wine, women and meat' was religiously followed in spite of many occasions that tested his resolve. In some instances, as Gandhiji often said that he was saved by Providence. However, what seems to override amongst all the circumstances was his inner voice that basically never wanted to be wronged.

One can scarcely say that Gandhiji had in-born natural leadership qualities. for, on many occasions in England, his reticence prevented him from communicating or expressing his opinion. However, this is not to say that he had no opinions at all. However, fear of failure and meagre exposure intimidated him. the turnaround of his persona happened in South Africa where he worked ceaselessly for the cause of the Indians and the natives.

The Maritzburg incident where Gandhiji was pushed out of the first class compartment for being a 'coolie barrister' caused an inner churning. It was indeed the fruition of mustering courage over reticence that spurred a will to continue to travel first class till Pretoria even after being ridiculed.

Gandhiji not only solved the case of Dada Abdulla and Tyabji amicably outside the court in Durban but also aided the formation of the Natal Indian Congress that stood up to the rights of indentured Indian labourers specifically and Indians generally in Transvaal and other regions of South Africa. Appeals entitled "Every Briton in South Africa" and "The Indian Franchise—An Appeal", the two pamphlets that were distributed to bring to light the conditions of the natives and Indians were received well. Taxes on Indian indentured labourers were reduced from £ 25 to a poll tax of £ 3 to finally being called off. These successes were the result of the sweat of combined labour, as the autobiography mentions, of the entire community and the Natal Indian Congress.

In India, the lethal weapons of *Satyagraha* and *Ahimsa* were used more vehemently than even in South Africa. The Indian freedom movement evolved from non-violent Non-Cooperation to Civil Disobedience to *Poorna Swaraj* and finally to *Swadeshi.*

In the collected essays in '*Mahatma Gandhi Essays and Reflections*' by Dr. Sarvepalli Radhakrishnan, Horace Alexander (*Mahatma Gandhi: An Estimate*) describes what Gandhiji said after his tour of the Indian countryside. One message that he wanted to give the English people was "to get off our backs". Alexander continued: "says Gandhiji, you must refuse to help him (the British rule) in any way while he remains where he is. And so, in the end, he must climb down. All his props and support have gone. He may threaten you with every kind of punishment if you do not continue to support him. He may carry out his threats...He cannot coerce you into action which your conscience tells you is wrong."

Frequent resorts to fasting, curtailing all extravagance and living a Spartan life, leading by example, were Gandhiji's trademark means to make sure he represented his deep convictions. A nation cast by divisive sentiments of caste and religion, living under the grim and instilled inferiority of being called 'barbaric' and 'uncivilised', with its women never being a part of the social reality but suffering its pang nonetheless, Gandhiji's politics have addressed these intertwined grievances.

In the same editorial work by Dr. Radhakrishnan mentioned earlier, an essay by Richard Gregg entitled '*Gandhiji as a Social Scientist and Social Inventor*', the author lists six major areas of social work by the 'Father of the Nation': poverty, unemployment, violence, factions and divisiveness between social groups, sanitation and agriculture. This included encouragement given to village industries especially cottage industries for providing relief to the seasonally unemployed, widespread dissemination of the value of cleanliness and *Swadeshi* movement. In the many letters Gandhiji wrote to the residents of *Satyagraha Ashram* from the Yeravada Prison, he writes on *Swadeshi* as, "greatest delusion to suppose, that the duty of *Swadeshi* begins and ends with merely spinning some yarn anyhow and wearing *Khadi* made from it...A votary of *Swadeshi* will carefully study his environment, and try to help his neighbours wherever possible...to reject foreign manufactures merely because they are foreign, and to go on wasting national time and money in promotion in one's country of manufactures for which it is not suited would be criminal folly, and a negation of the *Swadeshi* spirit."

Gandhiji's views on trusteeship are also well known. His ways may not seem radical when he says he desires the richer class or those possessing wealth not to pauperise themselves but to use wealth as trustees of the people. Yet, on a deeper plane, such a trusteeship is even more radical than the conventional demands on the wealth owning class, for trusteeship calls for an inner transformation. It requires one to cultivate the feeling of detachment. Gandhiji is observed addressing members of the '*Navajawan Sabha*' in 1931 as:

"If you want capital to be extinct or you want to abolish moneyed men or the capitalists, you will never succeed. What you must do is to demonstrate to the capitalists the power of labour and they will consent to be the trustees of those who toil for them...I want the rich to hold their riches in trust for the poor, or to give them up for them. Do you know that I gave up all my property when I founded Tolstoy Farm? Ruskin's *Unto this Last* inspired me, and I built my farm on those lines. You will now recognise that I am a foundation member of your Peasants' and Workers' Republic." (Desai, 2001: 67).

In terms of the politic-economic development strategy, he was far from the top-down governance approach of either the Capitalist or the Communist means of production. Development, from his perspective, called for an 'Appropriate Technology' that suited the resource endowment pattern, participative democracy, was sustainable, and slow in terms of growth yield but egalitarian. One could call his developmental approach to be in line with E.F Schumacher's '*Small Is Beautiful*'.

It is each one's own judgement as to how far was Gandhiji successful but what is commendable is the strength of faith in the same tools that most of the world reckons to be 'weakness'. Not being able to hit back, to most it is a sign of weakness. However, *Satyagraha* insists on not just passive tolerance but love and sympathy to those causing the hurt. the logic to this seemingly illogical behaviour is a deep understanding of the human psyche. It is only an ailing person that can cause the infection of his disease to spread. How can a person content and satiated hurt someone? He does not have the need to. Therefore, it is the sick, who, unaware of his own condition, displaces them onto others. The perpetrators of injustice are in reality, are a case of pity and not of anger. *Ahimsa* is a tool to make them understand their own illness and even balm them through compassion. Such men, who walk the path of this saintly wisdom, are far and fewer but are nonetheless apostles of truth and live by them untiringly.

The more one reads about his convictions and uniqueness, the more one is intrigued to know the source of it all. Of the three major influences, Gandhiji considers that of *Aram Krupalu Dev* to be the greatest. However, conventional literature has hardly pondered over these questions: Who was *Aram Krupalu Dev*? What was the relationship that they shared? How did the transformation take shape?

The Source: 'Raychandbhai'

'Raychandbhai'[1] or *Aram Krupalu Dev* was the son-in-law of one of the elder brothers of Dr. Mehta, Gandhiji's host when he returned to Bombay as a Barrister from London. He was an adept jeweller, a renowned poet and a '*shatavadhani*' an expert in the art of multi-tasking a hundred tasks simultaneously with utmost efficiency. His mental faculties were highly spoken of. However, more than the command over this rare intelligence, he was known for his equipoise, deep spiritual knowledge, truthfulness, compassion, courtesy and nothing short of constant yearning for being in the true state of the soul.

Gandhiji writes in his autobiography: "Raychandbhai's commercial transactions covered hundreds of thousands. He was a connoisseur of pearls and diamonds. No knotty business problem was too difficult for him. But, all these things were not the centre round which his life revolved. The centre was the passion to see God face to face. Amongst the things on his business table there were invariably to be found some religious book and his diary…The man who, immediately on finishing his talk about weighty business transactions, began to write about hidden things of the spirit could evidently not be a businessman at all, but a real seeker after Truth. And I saw him thus absorbed in godly pursuits in the midst of business, not once or twice, but very often."

Param Krupalu Dev's father Shri Ravjibhai was a Vaishnav and mother Smt. Devbaji was a Jain. He was born of devoutly religious parents. At about eleven years of age, he could explain deep spiritual meaning behind the sacred and revered epics of *Ramayana* and *Mahabharata*. Some of his major works include *Mokshamala, Bhavana Bodh*, Shree *Atma Siddhi Shastra*, varied spiritual poems and a collection of letters written to various liberation seekers compiled under the title 'Shrimad Rajchandra' (*Vachanamrutji*) by Shree Ambalal Bhai, a devotee of Shrimadji. Many of his works have been lost but seekers after truth take light, direction and strength from his existing profound words.

It was a relationship with such a highly noble soul that Gandhiji's inner journey took off. In one of the publications of Shrimad Rajchandra Ashram Agas, its President Bhulabhai V. Patel writes: "This association with Shrimadji, both in person and by correspondence has been very useful and beneficial to Gandhiji in the religious and spiritual matters."

Gandhiji met *Aram Krupalu Dev* only after he was back from England as a Barrister and it grew stronger in the two years of personal interaction from 1891 to 1893. He writes in his autobiography: "I was but a brief-less barrister then, and yet whenever I saw him he would engage me in conversation of a seriously religious nature. Though, I was groping and could not be said to have any serious interest in religious discussion, still I found his talk of absorbing interest. I have since met many a religious leader or teacher. I have tried to meet the heads of various faiths, and I must say that no one else has ever made on me the impression that Raychandbhai did."

It was *Aram Krupalu Dev's* guidance that gave Gandhiji solace in the vexing circumstances when he himself began questioning his religious inclination. A letter containing twenty seven questions on the nature of the soul, salvation, bondage, violence, Hindu scriptures etc., *Aram Krupalu Dev's* replies are both detailed and profound. Its impact on Gandhiji can be felt in the various ways he has responded to events occurring later in his life.

The very first question asked was: "What is the Soul?" In his reply on 20th October, 1894, Param Krupalu Dev explains using the principle of what the *Shastras* call '*Viveka*' or discrimination as the soul to be '*nitya*' or 'permanent' and the non-living entities like pot as '*anitya*' or ephemeral. The soul, that always exists, has no birth and no death and knowledge is its nature. Param Krupalu Dev writes in the letter mentioned above: "There is, therefore, no error or logical difficulty in believing that the *atman*, the existence of which is the cause of our experiencing happiness and suffering which also withdraws itself from either and which is conscious of something which thinks and impels, is characterised by awareness as its essential nature and that, in virtue of this nature, it is an imperishable entity which exists eternally; on the contrary, belief in the *atman* has the merit of accepting truth."

This explains a universal truth of the body being ephemeral and the soul being ever-lasting. the Truth that Gandhiji always strived for was this soul realisation or the self-realisation as opposed to the association of the self with the body or external objects. Simplicity, frugal living and '*Aparigraha*' or non-possession that we see in Bapu's life are the by-products of this belief. God realisation through Truth realization or Soul realisation is its result.

One amongst the twenty seven questions pertained to who is God and Shrimadji replied: "You, I and others are souls suffering the bondage of *karma*. The soul's existence in its natural state, that is, freedom from *karma* and purely as the *atman* that it is, is the state of being '*Ishvar*'." One can connect these words with what Gandhiji writes in '*Ashram Observances in Action*': "What is the vision of the Truth or God? It does not mean seeing something with the physical eye or witnessing a miracle. Seeing God means realization of the fact that God abides in one's heart. The yearning must persist until one has attained this realization, and will vanish upon realization. It is with this end in view that we keep observance, and engage ourselves in spiritual endeavour at the *Ashram*." The process of being free from the bondages of *karma* and disciplining oneself for getting closer to one's own self is exactly *Param Krupalu Dev's* instruction and Mahatma's life *mantra* or principle.

One such vow for self-discipline that Gandhiji strived very hard to achieve was '*Brahmacharya*' or celibacy. The definition he refers to is holistic. "*Charya* means course of conduct; *brahmacharya* conduct is adapted to the search of *Brahma*, i.e. Truth. From this etymological meaning arises the special meaning, viz. control of all the senses." (Gandhi, 1932:15). Gandhiji took the vow twice and had to break it. However, his indomitable will power persisted and it was taken finally with success in 1906 and he credits *Param Krupalu Dev* for the same in his autobiography: "I cannot definitely say what the circumstance or what book it was, that set my thoughts in that direction, but I have a recollection that the predominant factor was the influence of Raychandbhai".

Gandhiji's spiritual labour or *purushartha*, reflects sheer *bhákti* or devotion. There is never a false pride of achievement but an expression of gratitude and a sense of surrender to God. "His name and His Grace are the last resources of the aspirant after *Moksha*" (Gandhi 1927:177). One more trait that Gandhiji is known for is his secular approach to religion. *Ashram* residents of all castes and religions would observe the ritual of daily prayers without any discrimination against others. Bapu notes several incidents of a person of a religion accepting a devotional song belonging to other religions and such exchanges and interactions occurring not out of tolerance in the negative connotation but sharing out of a sense of brotherhood. "Rustomji Sheth very much liked the Gujarati *bhajan*, '*Mane Valun*', "Dear, dear to me is the name of Rama." If my memory serves me right, Maganlal or Kashi was once leading us in singing this hymn, when Rustomji Sheth exclaimed joyously, "Say the name of Hormazd instead of name of Rama." His suggestion was readily taken up, and after that whenever Sheth was present, and sometimes even when he was not, we put in the name of Hormazd in place of Rama. The late Husain, son of Daud Sheth, often stayed at the Phoenix *Ashram*, and enthusiastically joined our prayers. To the accompaniment of an organ, he used to sing in a very sweet voice the song *'Hai bahare bagh'*...Its inclusion in our *Bhajanavali* is a tribute to truth-loving Husain's memory" (Gandhi, 1932: 32).

This could be linked to Gandhiji's question to Shrimad on whether the Vedas were the roots of all religions and Shrimadji insisted: "it is only right that you and I and others should reflect and consider which of these systems of ideas has more power—truth—in them." These words in themselves were speaking loud about tolerance and sensitivity to differences in matters religious and mundane.

Conclusion

The aim of this essay is not to draw a forceful comparison between Gandhiji's life and principles and *Param Krupalu Dev's* teaching. In fact, it is to say that the two happen to link together very fluidly and naturally. The common thread between them is illumination of divinity which one at a higher pedestal is attempting to ignite in the other that is yearning for the same. Gandhiji's life is a mirror reflection of such ignition and illumination.

History is a witness to innumerable wars and the destruction it has caused to the victor and the vanquished alike but very few wars are fought against wrong deeds instead of wrong doers. In ancient times, if one won a war and respected the opponent, it was considered to be a sign of true statesmanship. Here, true statesmanship quality is not something that arises after the war is won. It is realised much before that since the war is fought with sheer compassion and self-sacrifice.

This not only curtails the divisions of anger and hatred between the warring entities but also avoids the transaction costs of long and arduous litigation and physical loss of life and property. An ethical leader, besides, also sets an example for discouraging rent seeking activities in the state and promotes policies for harmonious and long term welfare of its citizenry. Through the anecdotal case study of the relationship between Gandhiji and *Param Krupalu Dev*, it becomes abundantly clear that ethics and morality helps transform individuals and nations altogether. For the State to have Good Governance practices and for it to run a democracy in its truest sense, where is there a way except the one which ethics and morality pave?

Note

1. The word 'Raychandbhai' has been used purposely here since it is the title of a chapter in Gandhiji's autobiography.

References

Bhattacharya Sabyasachi, (Ed.) (2014) The *Mahatma and the Poet: Letters and Debates between Gandhi and Tagore, 1915-1941.* New Delhi: National Book Trust.

Desai, Kalpana (2001) *Compilations: The Mahatma beyond Gandhi,* Mumbai Sarvodaya International Trust, Maharashtra Chapter.

Dr. Radhakrishnan, Sarvepalli, (Ed.) (2015) *Mahatma Gandhi: Essays and Reflections,* Jaico Publishing House.

Gandhi, M. K. (1927), *An Autobiography* Or *The Story of My Experiments with Truth,* Ahmedabad: Navjivan Publishing House.

Gandhi, M.K. (1955a) *Ashram Observances in Action*, Ahmedabad: Navjivan Publishing House.

Gandhi, M.K., (1932), *From Yeravada Mandir,* Ahmedabad: Navjivan Publishing House.

Gandhi, M.K., (1955b), *My Religion,* Ahmedabad: Navjivan Publishing House.

Shrimad Rajchandra Charitra Jeevan Darshan (Shrimad Rajchandra Janma Bhavan, Vavania: 2001).

Shrimad Rajchandra's Reply to Gandhiji's Questions, Shrimad Rajchandra Ashram, Agas, 2000.

Thompson Mel, (2003), *Ethical Theory,* Hodder and Stoughton.

Tikekar, S.R. (1971), *Epigrams from Gandhiji,* New Delhi: Publications Divisions, Ministry of Information and Broadcasting, Government of India.

Index